"Duar [...] decline of the mainline churches is worthy of the attention of serious students of religion in America. His projection for the future of Christianity in the United States is both concerning and hopeful. His explanation of factors related to the possibility of détente between the churches of the Christian right and the mainline churches may be seen as groundbreaking. The reader will be led to rethink some of his/her own convictions, tradition, and practices."

Rt. Rev. Jon Bruno
Bishop Diocesan
Episcopal Diocese of Los Angeles

"Dr. Day examines the growth of the fundamentalist, evangelical, and Gnostic organizations and compares them with the decline of the traditional mainline denominations. He answers the question 'What can mainline church leaders learn from this transition without forgoing their own historic roots?' He also illustrates the serious difficulties within the rapidly growing groups. Dr. Day's explorations have serious political ramifications."

Rev. Dianna Pohlman Bell
Forty years a Presbyterian Minister
First Woman United States Military Chaplain (Navy)

"As one who grew up in the conservative Christian and evangelical church and college, this book helped fill in the gaps of my knowledge and understanding of mainline churches and more. Dr. Day's writing is informative and challenging providing a comprehensive perspective on the American church landscape. I do not agree with all that he posits, but he made me think about and see things in a new way."

Len Hightower, PhD
Principal
HighTower Consulting

GOD'S ESTABLISHMENT

GOD'S ESTABLISHMENT
What Happened?

DUANE L. DAY

TATE PUBLISHING *& Enterprises*

God's Establishment
Copyright © 2011 by Duane L. Day. All rights reserved.

No part of this publication may be reproduced, stored in a retrieval system or transmitted in any way by any means, electronic, mechanical, photocopy, recording or otherwise without the prior permission of the author except as provided by USA copyright law.

Scripture quotations are from The New English Bible, The Delegates Of The Oxford University Press And The Syndics Of The Cambridge University Press, 1961, 1970. Used by permission. All rights reserved.

The opinions expressed by the author are not necessarily those of Tate Publishing, LLC.

Published by Tate Publishing & Enterprises, LLC
127 E. Trade Center Terrace | Mustang, Oklahoma 73064 USA
1.888.361.9473 | www.tatepublishing.com

Tate Publishing is committed to excellence in the publishing industry. The company reflects the philosophy established by the founders, based on Psalm 68:11,
"The Lord gave the word and great was the company of those who published it."

Book design copyright © 2011 by Tate Publishing, LLC. All rights reserved.
Cover design by Kellie Southerland
Interior design by Joel Uber

Published in the United States of America

ISBN: 978-1-61346-098-6
1. Religion; Christianity, General
2. Religion; Christian Church, Growth
11.06.21

Dedicated to Charmaine
and Deborah, Rebecca, Kevin, Patricia, Debra

Acknowledgments

I want to acknowledge my debt in the writing of this book to the Reverend Canon Bradford Karelius, the Reverend Donald Bell, and the Honorable Rich Vogl. In my research, I had occasion to interview and/or observe a number of persons who are representative of one of the communities of faith examined in this book. Among them, several stand out for their faith and their commitment of time to this project: Barbara Shirley, Allen and Pamela Galera, Mel Rogers, and the men and women who participated in a class I taught entitled "What Happened to the Mainline Church?" The Tate Publishing staff has been skillful and professional in their dealings with me. I am especially grateful for the attention to detail and the suggestions my editor, Sabrina Arndt, has offered.

My secretary for many years, Cathy Umeda, continued, somehow, to make sense of my handwriting. My sister-in-law, Julie Holguin, helped immeasurably in preparing the book for publication. My son, Kevin, was the source of inestimable support. And this work, as so many of my other efforts across the years, would never have been possible without the encouragement and insight of my wife, Charmaine.

All of you—friends, supporters, and critics—have made this a better book.

To all who affirm that Jesus is Lord, including those of you who may disagree with me on some issues, I pray for you and wish for you God's rich blessings. May God grant you both comfort and challenge.

Table of Contents

Prologue

For a dozen years, I sputtered over the fact that the clergy most frequently quoted in the media or the churches whose ministries are highlighted in the press have been representative of the Christian right. Fundamentalists and evangelicals seem to be found in churches labeled nondenominational or Bible or Calvary or some non-definitive description like Willow Creek, Mariners, or Saddleback. Such names appear to them to be more welcoming, more open than St. Mark's Episcopal or First Presbyterian. They are the ones deemed more newsworthy.

Annoyed by the apparent refusal of the press and the electronic media to identify and quote the local United Church of Christ pastor or the Evangelical Lutheran cleric, I complained to my wife that the reporters and anchormen had to be ignorant about religion to indulge in so clear a bias for the right. She set me straight: "There are a lot more people in the fundamentalist churches than there are in the churches like the Methodists and Presbyterians." Her information was based on the attitudes and apparent commitments of the college students she teaches.

"No," I insisted, "those students are not representative. The right has co-opted the press."

I was wrong! When my frustration led me to check the numbers, I was dumbstruck to find that the mainline churches[1] today could claim only 12 percent of church membership in the United States (Another study I found used 18 percent for the mainline denomination's share of current church members. The difference may be accounted for by disagreement over churches of which denominations can rightly be called mainline.) However that matter is settled, it is clear that the churches of historic Protestantism have lost their once-clear leadership standing and become marginal—at least in terms of influence, number of adherents, and resources they can rightly claim.

I grew up in an American Baptist Church[2]—conservative but not rigidly so. Later, I was pastor of a Congregational Church, soon to become part of the United Church of Christ. Still later, I settled into an inner-city Episcopal Church. Aside from the fact that the services of worship in which I now participate are liturgical and those in years past were not, the churches with which I have been affiliated shared certain char-

---

1 The term *mainline church* is, admittedly, inexact or, perhaps more accurately, flexible. It usually includes Methodists, Presbyterians, Episcopalians, United Church of Christ, Disciples of Christ, American Baptists, and the Evangelical Lutheran Church in America.

2 The American Baptist Church of my childhood also was the church in which Tim LaHaye, one of the authors of the *Left Behind* series, was a member. The church was in Dearborn, Michigan. We were both members of Boy Scout Troop FS2. Tim left Michigan to attend Bob Jones University; I got my undergraduate degree at Wayne University (now Wayne State) and my professional and graduate degrees from Andover Newton Theological School and Union Theological Seminary.

acteristics; they were churches of historic Protestant-ism—mainline churches.

Although I served as a pastor for some eight years and was a UCC bureaucrat for four years, most of my career has been spent as an academic. I can't point to thirty years as a pastor. I can, however, claim many years of active life in local churches with some denominational and ecumenical responsibilities along the way.

When I discovered the stunning decline of membership and influence that marked the mainline churches, I found myself seeking explanations: Were the mainline churches once as dominant as I remembered, or am I making that up? If they were, why did all the people leave? Assuming those departing members continued to have some religious impulse, where did they go? Will the mainline churches rise again? Can they?

The reader has a right to know where I stand as together we look at what happened to what I have called "God's Establishment." It will be clear that my own Christian faith has been shaped by churches that were, or are, at one level or another, establishment churches. My view of the Bible is that it can best be understood by an approach that is sometimes called "higher criticism"—the historical/literary approach. That approach does not correspond to the view of any of the groups represented in chapters three through seven of this work, but it preserves the idea that the Judaeo-Christian scriptures are important and are accessible to reason.

You will note that my view of the appropriate role of the Christian Church in American life differs in many respects from the churches of the Christian right and the modern-day Gnostics. Their right-bearing political agenda seems to me to be discriminatory and closed-minded and, therefore, unworthy of those who confess Jesus as Lord. There are encouraging signs that I salute—signs that indicate growing numbers of evangelicals are taking seriously their responsibility to meet the earthly needs of the poor, the ill, the hungry, and the prisoner.

The commitment that drives my faith is not to an afterlife that is free from hell's fire but to a here-and-now life of generosity of spirit, a community of caring, and love for my fellow man. Such a life, I would submit, is one that Jesus would have us live.

So we're different: Those whose version of Christianity has captured many former mainline church members and me. Those who have made of the Bible an icon against which people can be measured and your author. Those who attended Bob Jones and this person who studied at Andover Newton and Union. Despite those differences, I have tried to be fair and accurate in summarizing the history, commitments, and practices of those described in chapters three through seven.

Preface

This work was conceived as a "wake-up call" to the clergymen and women of the churches of historic Protestantism and to the committed laymen and lay-women who support and provide leadership to those churches. These have not been easy years for you, no matter the scholarship, effort, and conviction that have gone into your ministries. The movement most of your churches have experienced over the last three or four decades has been retrograde. It is also directed to those interested in religion and to individuals who are puzzled by the direction United States Protestantism seems to have taken in recent years.

There is a church located in a judicatory I once led for my denomination that had, on a recent Sunday morning, a worship attendance of thirty-five! It is a church whose building is an architectural gem, where preaching was once king, whose staff once boasted six full-time members in addition to section leaders in the chancel choir, whose membership was comprised of officials in government and in the schools and colleges in the region, and whose outreach ministries were addressed to real community needs and were of high quality and innovative. Thirty-five!

Another church, one I did not personally know, was the site of the recent funeral of a retired clergyman with whom I had once worked. When I learned of his death, I called the church to inquire about the phone numbers of his family that I might make contact to express my sympathy. The call provided me with an electronic message: "This is XX church. The church office is open, and this telephone is answered Thursday afternoons from 1:00 p.m. to 5:00 p.m. Please leave your message." I did leave a message. My call was never returned. Can you imagine a church of a mainline denomination in a suburban community whose telephone is answered four hours a week?

There is a former mainline church in the suburban city in which I now live that has been converted into a white-tablecloth restaurant. My wife and I dine there.

What happened? What, in the name of God, happened?

The answer is clear and it is stark: large numbers of members have walked away from the churches of the mainline denominations. What is less clear is the answer to the question "Why did they leave?" And to the question "What can or should the churches of the mainline denominations do about their decline?" The answers at this point would appear to be moot.

This book explores, at some length, the "why did they leave?" conundrum:

- Differing political views held by the clergy and the members of their congregations.

- Urbanization and the resulting movement of members to the suburbs.

- The failure or inability of the mainline churches to "speak the languages" of the young and the consequent departure of young people and their parents.

- Clergy ineffectiveness.

- The lack of standards, discipline, and authority in the mainline churches.

- The failure to be faithful to the proclamation of the gospel message.

Those who left these churches did not all embrace irreligion. Rather, to a remarkable degree, they searched for a congregation with which they could identify and in which they could find meaning. A lot of them, perhaps most of them, turned right. There is no gainsaying the fact that the fundamentalist and evangelical churches and their allies, the Pentecostalists and Charismatics, are the answer to the question "What's happening now?" on America's religious front.

Other former mainline church members have made their way to one or another of the groups labeled here, modern-day Gnostics, for the reason that they—as their nominal forbearers—claim to possess knowledge that other Christians do not possess. Their "secrets" have proved convincing to some erstwhile mainline church folk. The three of them discussed here—the Church of Jesus Christ of Latter-day Saints (Mormons), Jehovah's Witnesses, and Seventh-day Adventists—are aggressive in their evangelistic efforts. Their faithful may be seen on the streets of cities and towns across the length and breadth of the nation spreading their understanding of the good news. And all have had significant, and in some measure, unexpected success.

I hope those mainline clergy and lay leaders who turn to this work will expand their knowledge about their competition. Knowledge may lead to understanding. Understanding may be the base from which critical operational decisions can be reached and implemented.

- Do the mainline churches want or need to show institutional growth? Is that their most urgent priority, or do we believe our calling is to proclaim the gospel of justice, community, and peace, whatever the cost?

- Are there tactics or behaviors to be learned and adopted from the Christian churches that are growing?

- To what degree does intellect and reason shape the message we proclaim?

- Are there bridges we should build to Christian brothers and sisters who are currently outside the mainline?

- Jesus' ministry was directed to the outcasts, the poor, the sick, the prisoners. Has our constituency—the establishment—diminished the authenticity of our message? If so, how should we deal with a disconnect between constituency and message?

- What should we be asking of our members? With what must we provide them if their, and our, discipleship is to prove effective and welcoming?

- Can the churches of the mainline regain strength and operational vitality by focusing efforts on and ministering to immigrant populations?

- Some mainline churches have begun to emphasize such spiritual disciplines as contemplative prayer and intercessory prayer. Others have moved ministry in the direction of personal transformation. Will such emphases help the mainline regain its soul?

There are, of course, other questions to be posed and answers to be sought. What seems clear is that this is not the time for the churches of the mainline to hunker down, to continue doing and saying what has already been said and done, even as change is shaping a new present and future. Is it too much to say that God is again calling the mainline churches, calling for faithfulness of a dimension that is significantly deeper and more profound than that which marked the mainline churches in the recent past?

Back in the Day

The years immediately following World War II saw the flourishing of the churches of the historic Protestant denominations in the United States. Memberships grew to previously unimagined numbers. Attendance at the weekly services of worship regularly reached, and often surpassed, 40 percent of membership. Sunday schools were packed with kids *and* adults. Budgets for local operating expenses and missions reached numbers heretofore thought unreachable.

Seminaries were crowded due, in part, to the funds afforded by the GI Bill, making study for the ministry—or almost anything else, for that matter—affordable. And it should not be forgotten that the extremities of combat endured by the men in the wartime military led more than a few to consider a Christian vocation an obligation they had to meet. There were, it was said, "no atheists in foxholes."

Across the nation, churches were building larger sanctuaries and Sunday school additions. New churches were being planted in new housing tracts. Denominations purchased large plots of land in outlying areas on which they planned to build facilities to house their summer camps.

It was the rare Christian congregation that did not have a "building campaign" in the period from 1946 to 1960. Indeed, a surprising number mounted two or more such campaigns in that decade and a half. Fundraising firms grew fat from the fees earned raising money from the faithful for new church buildings. And there were architects who did nothing but design new church facilities. Pew and chancel furniture manufacturers thrived!

Church youth groups attracted even the popular kids—football players, members of the homecoming courts, the casts of the school plays. The summer camps of the mainline denominations frequently had to call off summer registrations *before* federal income tax day.

The daily press paid attention to the mainline churches. As a matter of course, metropolitan dailies had one or more religion editors/writers on staff. Monday editions of the papers summarized sermons in major articles and promoted the music and education offerings of selected churches. *Time* and *Newsweek* and the general interest publications (*Saturday Evening Post*, *Life*, *Look*, and others) paid close attention to what was happening in the churches and wrote long stories, complete with pictures.

Radio had long tipped its hat to the church; from the 1930s onward, the networks had committed programming (primarily, but not exclusively, on Sundays) to prominent Protestant preachers—Harry Emerson Fosdick, Ralph Sockman, George Buttrick, Norman Vincent Peale. And in the years after the war, television executives made airtime available, free of charge, throughout the year and on special occasions to clerics—most, if not all, were representative of the mainline churches.

Local media took their cue from the national press. It was rare to find even a small city whose newspapers were not "all over" the religious beat. And local radio and television committed more than a few of their broadcast hours to the churches and clergymen in their service areas.

Growth was not the domain solely of the mainline Protestant churches, so extensive media attention was given not only to the Presbyterians and Methodists. The Catholics had a media superstar in Monsignor, then bishop, then Archbishop Fulton J. Sheen, whose on-air homilies earned his program, *Life is Worth Living*, a primetime slot on one of the national networks.[1] By the 1950s the national media had commenced paying attention to religious personages on the right—first, Billy Graham, and a bit later, Oral Roberts, and, on the regional and local scene, many others.

The apparent triumph of the mainline church now seems a vestige of the distant past. The growth dynamic, for the present, resides with the fundamentalist and evangelical churches. By way of illustration, the megachurch phenomenon—huge congregations with massive campuses providing a range of on-site services from uniformed parking attendants to credit unions to Starbucks—is, by a wide margin, to be found on the right of the United States Christian spectrum.

In a remarkable turnabout, the media now give less than passing attention to the mainline church. Even a casual reading of the dailies will reveal that they appear to see the American religious scene in thirds: Roman Catholics, fundamentalists/evangelical and ethnic churches and clergy. One looks in vain for media coverage about Episcopalians, for example, unless something has happened or a statement has been made that deals with homosexuality or the ordination of women. Mainline Protestantism, and the ministries of the churches thus identified, has all but vanished from the public stage.

The numbers seem to answer the question "Why?" From 1960 to 2009, there has been a steep and continuing drop in the percentage of the total population who claim to be in one of the seven denominations usually identified as mainline. The actual numbers are startling:[2]

	1960	2009
Methodists	10,641,310	7,931,733
Presbyterians (USA)	4,161,880	2,941,412
Episcopalians	3,269,325	2,116,749
United Church of Christ	2,241,134	1,111,691
American Baptists	1,521,052	1,358,351
Evangelical Lutheran Church in America	5,295,502	4,709,956
Disciples of Christ	1,801,414	1,071,616

Given the trend, it's no wonder that mainline Protestantism is largely ignored by the media. It's as though the historic denominations have simply ceased to be.

"We don't give attention to the Stanley Steamer automobile either," one media-type snorted.

There are several reasons for the current state of affairs. Those reasons are explored, at length, in chapter eight. Preliminarily, it should be noted that many of their members reasoned that the mainline churches changed the rules in midstream for those who filled the pews in the years following World War II. They were looking for an institution that would undergird family life by implementing programs to serve the family and keep the kids busy: preschools, Sunday schools, youth groups, confirmation classes, summer camps, work projects in poor communities, preferably in exotic locales. Those were all perceived to be "good things," and Mom and Dad could feel that their church membership, preferably in a congregation of like-minded persons, proved that they were good people doing good things. And that membership usually meant a friendship cohort of fellow Christians who were upwardly mobile, well dressed, and obvious pillars of the community.

Then came the 1960s, and everything changed. The civil rights revolution burst on the scene. The Reverend Dr. Martin Luther King, Jr., a graduate of two seminaries with mainline church affiliations, demonstrated and preached in support of heretofore denied rights for the nation's African American population. He won the approbation and support of a significant portion (not all) of the clergy of the mainline churches. It was not long before the front pages and the airwaves were filled with pictures of preachers sitting in, marching, and engaging in acts of civil disobedience in support of African Americans.

Sunday sermons denouncing segregation tied the civil rights message to the words and spirit of Jesus of Nazareth. While religious leaders, other than those of mainline Protestantism, could be found giving support to the cause of civil rights, it was the African American and mainline clergy who furnished the bulk of the civil rights leadership[3].

At about the same time, the president with roots in Texas, Lyndon B. Johnson, prodded the Congress of the United States to join him in a "war on poverty." Head Start programs were mounted, supported by government funds, for the poorest Americans—usually African American, often Hispanic. Community organization efforts were instituted to challenge a status quo that seemed to deny opportunities for the poor to climb out of poverty. Churches and churchmen, though not all, jumped on board and supported, in word and deed, the struggle to erase poverty in the United States. One-fifth of America living below the poverty line became a mantra repeated again and again from mainline pulpits across the nation. Parishioners were told that the gospel demanded an end to poverty. The words of Jesus about the poor, the hungry, the prisoner were quoted in support of activity in the war on poverty. It was not that the fundamentalists and evangelicals declared *for* poverty; rather, the message from pulpits of the Christian right focused on salvation and the life that awaited the saved in heaven. The poor would be rewarded richly in the afterlife provided only that they confessed Jesus as Lord and Savior.

Then came the Vietnam War. Early involvement of the United States in the struggle produced little dissent; the attitude that we didn't want the communists to win was common—a clear majority attitude. But as time passed, U.S. troop deployments grew and casualties skyrocketed. Growing numbers of Americans determined that this was a war from which we had to extricate ourselves. "It's a civil war and none of our business" began to be heard from the pulpit with growing frequency and increasing vehemence. Once again, among the outspoken were mainline clergy who argued for troop withdrawal and the conversion of military funding to the nation's social needs. The National Council of Churches, with a base larger than the mainline denominations but heavily dependent on those churches for funding and leadership, spoke—sometimes with strident voice—about the evil of U.S. involvement and the necessity of peace.

The man and woman in the pew—or at least many of them—grew uncomfortable with what they were hearing from the pulpit. Civil rights and the defeat of poverty and an end to the Vietnam War were not the issues that had drawn them into the church in the first place; it was about family values and kids and feeling good and being good. Now those in the pew were being told over and over again that there were problems in this nation that demanded and deserved the attention of Christian men and women. Churchmen and churchwomen were being told that they were personally responsible for creating the status quo and that they had an obligation to make things better. "Preachers should stay out of politics" became a theme recited again and again by members of mainline churches in the 1960s and 1970s. Thus began the exodus.

The exodus happened to coincide in time, more or less, with the escalating rate of urbanization. The people pouring into the nation's cities were often African American or Hispanic and usually they were poor. In short order those who migrated into America's inner cities created social, cultural, and religious institutions that spoke to and represented them and their interests. They may (or may not) have tried the established institutions and found them wanting. Memberships in mainline city churches, almost totally white, declined, often precipitously. Financial support from communicants similarly shrank. With empty pews came empty offering plates. Membership down, attendance down, budgets down, the churches faced limited choices: One, they could mount programs aimed at attracting and serving the populations at hand; two, they could move their ministries to other, presumably more promising, locations; or three, they could close the doors.

Many, if not most, of the impacted congregations chose option one and courageously sought to minister to the population in the communities in which they were located. And some were successful in doing so. They were, largely, congregations that had sources of funds of sufficient size to finance activities and services that were not self-supporting. These activities often consisted of funding for additional staff outside of the "traditional" staff of clergy—for example, teachers, church athletic teams, and other youth leaders. It is the rare city that cannot point to one or more churches of a mainline denomination with vibrant ministries, serving a diverse membership, in the heart of the city. But that, in a sense, is the point; where once there were a dozen or more mainline churches in a particular urban setting, the exodus meant that the dozen became one or two.

In an ironic twist that would challenge the storytelling skill of a novelist, many of the churches that had opted to move to a near-in suburb are finding that their suburb is now facing a changing population and reduced memberships and revenue. Some of the population moving back to the city and suburbs are also experiencing changing demographics. The moveable church may once again travel.

To summarize, the growth of mainline Protestantism in the late forties, fifties, and early sixties was built upon programming that supported the classic family model: Mom and Dad together in an intact marriage, with Dad serving as the provider, and the kids being lovingly prepared by the churches to replicate that family model. Two of the slogans from those years betray the way in which the family interests metamorphosed into the Christian story: "Churchgoing families are happier families" and "Families that pray together, stay together." In the sixties and seventies, mainline churches, led by liberal clergy, adopted an activist posture on the pressing social/political issues of the day. A not inconsiderable number of heretofore loyal church members were angered, reasoning that they had been the victims of a bait and switch tactic—"You got me by supporting family values. Now you want me to have a black family living next door to me" and "Don't tell me, from the pulpit, that it is my responsibility to welcome black neighbors. Every penny I have is tied up in my house, and when *they* move in, I'll lose it all." And while this was playing out—to the detriment of the mainline church—the demographics of urban neighborhoods changed, and many white families—huge numbers—quite literally ran to the suburbs.

The mainline churches faced a hard reality: their people had moved away from the congregations in which they held their membership. It might seem logical to suppose that when they arrived in their new community, a solid Presbyterian family would seek out and affiliate with a Presbyterian church. Some of that—a lot of that—happened, of course. But one of the realities of life in the late twentieth century was that institutional loyalties tended to be rather shallower than they had been in earlier times. The move "farther out" often meant that a churchgoing family could feel freed from the ties that bound them to one tradition. They could look around to see what was out there—and look they did. Some simply gave up on the church, any church, but growing members found that there were churches that seemed to have a firmer grasp on their need and their politics than the one to which they had formerly belonged. Moreover, these churches seemed to have a lot more fun.

Churches in Conflict

Members of mainline churches who left their neighborhoods and their congregations in the late sixties, seventies, and eighties (and who continue to leave) chose a perplexing variety of destinations: Some sought out and affiliated with a church of the same denomination as the one they had left; some gave up entirely on churches, though they insisted that they continued to be "spiritual"; some admitted to a growing skepticism about religious faith and allowed that they had become atheists or at least agnostics; some became intrigued by the latter-day Gnostics; and many, in growing numbers, attached themselves to a fundamentalist or evangelical church—a church of the Christian right.

Many, perhaps a majority, of the churches of the Christian right are a suburban phenomenon. Marked by a dynamic that is palpable, memberships, staffs, and budgets are in remarkable growth mode. While some are centered in buildings that are clearly ecclesiastical in both design and purpose, others are located in facilities that were once factories, warehouses, or retail spaces. (It is amazing how some folding chairs set in rows with a center aisle and a table centered in front can transform even the dullest concrete-walled room into a church.)

Preachers in these churches are often judged to be undereducated or naïve about Judaeo-Christian scriptures, theology, and ethics—and many are! In fact, fundamentalist and evangelical leaders are often intelligent and articulate even as they reject or question much of modern learning. They are sensitive to and savvy about contemporary culture. They know pop, rock, and hip-hop. They understand electronic media. They raise "informal" to the level of a mandated rubric. They have learned skills at touching others' emotions, and they employ those skills.

The message proclaimed by the clergy of the Christian right focuses on salvation, heaven and hell, and Christ as a sacrifice for the individual's sins. In a word, their purpose is to evangelize, seeking to bring their listeners to a decision for Christ and against the devil! They want their followers to be born again. Failing to accept Christ as Lord and Savior, they insist, will mean hell and eternal damnation as punishment for sin. The clergy buy airtime on radio and television to spread their message. They preach in the quads and the dorms of colleges and universities[4] and on the street corners in cities and suburbs. And the people respond!

Megachurches are among the phenomena created by the Christianity of the right—local churches with weekly attendance of two thousand and more and memberships numbering five thousand, ten thousand, twenty thousand, and more. They are churches with coffee shops and hamburger franchises on site, churches with video screens located throughout the premises so that wherever a member happens to be on-site, he or she can see and/or hear the preacher and the musicians or read the message of the sermon preached most recently. They are churches with rock bands and some with full orchestras, churches singing not the grand, rich music of the Reformation and the Enlightenment but the ditties that characterize so-called "praise" (sometimes spelled Pray-Z) music.[5] They are churches that have public relations directors on staff and lawyers and makeup artists. They are churches that protect their pastors with bodyguards and churches, in short, that seem to resemble a Hollywood studio more than they do a center for worship. And rather than classic, recognizable worship, they are churches that appear as though they are there to entertain!

Of course, not all of the churches of the right are megachurches. Indeed, most are relatively small, 150 to 300 members, making do with a one-man preaching staff and a high school kid playing drums alongside a piano player from the congregation. The aspiration persists: to fill the house and seek the conversion of sinners and their salvation from the fires of hell that surely await the unfortunate who have not been born again.

The growth of the Christian right is very much in keeping with the theme and style of Christian history in North America. It sometimes appears that religion in America has been a two-step dance: first, establishment churches emphasizing the role of reason in faith; second, preachers proclaiming a religion of emotion. The latter characterizes the churches of the Christian right today.

And it was what characterized the Great Awakening of the eighteenth century. Commencing in 1726 in and around the area of New Brunswick, New Jersey, under the leadership of Reformed Churchman Theodore Frelinghuysen, the Great Awakening sought to awaken the people to the possibility of having a direct, personal experience with Christ. Revival broke out in New Jersey: conversions took place; church memberships grew; religious emotionalism became intense. Some clergy, Presbyterians among them, were uncomfortable with the more extreme manifestations of revival, and Presbyterianism split—the rupture was to last for decades. One was representing an experience with Christ while the other side represented the religion of reason.

The great English preacher George Whitfield toured the country, preaching the need for conversion. The famed Puritan cleric Jonathan Edwards was drawn to the cause; New England became a venue for the evangelical experience. The southern states were "on fire" with the emotion produced by revival. It has been reported that Benjamin Franklin was caught up in the emotion engendered by Whitfield's preaching and made a gift of money that surprised even Franklin for its generosity.

The Great Awakening lasted for some fifty years, only to see much of its energy "drained off" in the years of the American Revolution.

By the year 1800, experiential religion was riding high again in a movement that came to be known as the Second Great Awakening. Those who stood against this tide were Congregationalists who came to be called Unitarians and who held to the idea of salvation by character. They separated themselves from the main body of Congregationalists who responded by founding the first graduate school of theology in the United States, Andover Theological Seminary.[6] Harvard became Unitarian. The leaders of the Second Great Awakening were determined to avoid the excesses of the earlier Great Awakening: the revivals were more restrained and tended to take place within the normal patterns of church life.

Missionary societies were formed and missionaries sent out to far places. In the South, "camp meetings" were promoted, and the revivals equaled those of the earlier Great Awakening in their intensity and emotionalism. A young New York attorney, Charles Finney, led "splendid" revivals marked by his fervent, emotional preaching. Finney, as evangelicals today, believed that the central purpose of the church and its teaching was salvation.[7]

The Second Great Awakening left its mark in the form of growing Methodist and Baptist churches in the South, a safer American frontier, and communities of professing Christians in far-flung places. The soldiers on both sides in the Civil War were, more often than not, products of the Second Great Awakening.

In the years following the Civil War, the Christian right was represented by such men as itinerant evangelists Dwight Moody and Billy Sunday. Evolution and biblical criticism were rejected; mission work, at home and abroad, to the end of personal conversion and salvation was promoted; tent revival meetings were made possible by a growing highway system. Such was the nature of much of America Protestantism until after World War II.

Many among the leaders of the Christian right today argue that what they represent is America's Third Great Awakening. And if motive is to be counted—followers who have had a conversion experience—they may be correct. But if the all-too-real moral and ethical lapses of some of the prominent leaders of the Christian right are to be counted, if political appetites and aims are to be counted, if lavish lifestyles of preachers are to be counted, they may be wrong. Fervor may be there, and emotion, but the pristine morals and ethics of the leaders of the First and Second Great Awakening seem to be lacking in at least some of the highly publicized leaders of the Christian right.

Among the victories of the Christian right is the growth in the numbers of clergy of the mainline denominations who are adopting the tactics of the evangelicals. Established congregations are finding increasing numbers of clergy who are prepared to feature "praise" music, insist on having media screens at the front of the nave and in the narthex, and choose to get rid of traditional or ecclesiastically-related garb to preach and pray tieless and in shirt sleeves in the belief that by so doing they will be more accessible to young families.

In the preceding chapter, attention was directed to the predominance of the mainline churches in the fifties and sixties. In truth, historic Protestant Christianity was understood to be the dominant expression of the Christian faith in America from the very beginning in colonial days.

The names—Cotton Mather, Roger Williams, Jonathan Edwards, Alexander Campbell, Henry Ward Beecher, Phillips Brooks—were clerical expressions of mainstream Christian thought and practice known by many and were leaders who exerted remarkable influence on the nation. The churchly institutions of the mainstream—Old North Church, Trinity Church, the National Cathedral, Riverside Church, Fifth Avenue Presbyterian all bespoke a special place in America's history for mainstream Christianity. The Christian faithful who gave birth to movements that helped shape the nation—abolition, women's rights, the prohibition of child labor, civil rights, gay rights—are expressions of the aspirations for justice and opportunity for all. The institutions of learning that had their roots in mainstream Christianity—Harvard, Yale, Princeton, of course, and the University of Chicago, Vanderbilt, Rice, SMU, and Morehouse—were ones in which generation after generation of America's leaders had their talents and their commitments shaped and made ready for service in the public square.

It is that rich history, that plethora of gifts, that is being drained off as the mainline churches lose members, resources, confidence, and allies. The fundamentalist and evangelical churches, by contrast, appear to be growing on all fronts; their confidence in a winning future has reached the point at which they can tolerate—even support—Jim Wallis's call to social action, Rick Warren's invitation to the mainline to "come-on-over," Joel Osteen's prosperity gospel, and Mark Driscoll's macho Calvinism.

It remains for us to identify some of the common characteristics of America's mainline churches. Your understanding of those characteristics may differ from mine. These seem to me to be telling.

1. The mainline churches are all ecumenical. That does not mean, nor does it intend to imply, that the seven subject denominations are all equally committed to church mergers or a common institutional structure. It does mean that the members and leaders of these churches are willing to talk to and collaborate with other Christians—those in, out, or close to the mainstream.

2. These denominations all insist on an educated clergy. College or university graduation and three years or more in a graduate

theological school are the standard expectations of these churches for ordination.

3. All of the denominations of the mainline have oversight requirements of their clergy. The specific nature of the requirements differ from one denomination to another but are aimed at recognizing that ordination to ministry in a given denomination also has a "whole church" dimension, especially as it relates to safeguarding morality and ethics.

4. The churches in these denominations recognize and accept the content, if not the particular words, of the classic Creeds of Christendom—i.e., the Nicene Creed and the Apostles' Creed. Interpretations of the creeds may differ, even the understanding of the need for creeds may vary, but the beliefs articulated all fall within the range of Christian orthodoxy when it comes to the person and nature of Christ Jesus and the triune God.

5. While the churches of the seven denominations may have differing social outlooks, all would agree that the Christian gospel is to be acted out in society; war and peace, rich and poor, male and female, sick and well all have implications for faith and ministry.

6. These churches have a near-common hymnody that is utilized in public worship. That

hymnody draws on the riches of the music of the Reformation but does not reject more recent musical expressions of the faith.

7. The mainline churches celebrate both baptism and the Lord's Supper. For some, baptism is for believers only (American Baptists and Disciples of Christ), but for all, baptism marks entrance into Christ's church. The Lord's Supper varies in detail by denomination, but all recognize it as a time when God's grace may uniquely be visited upon his faithful people.

8. It would be wrong to say that the mainline churches have no political agenda; their agenda may oppose restrictions on homosexuals, on abortion, on stem cell research, and on the teaching of evolution. Such matters as environmental health, equal opportunity for all, and feeding the hungry are a positive focus.

9. From the pulpits of the seven denominations, one is likely to hear the gospel message couched in terms of community, the abundant life, and God's love rather than salvation from hell's eternal fire.

It is surely the case that many Christians in the mainstream will take exception to this list of common characteristics of the mainline churches. And it is true that each of the mainstream denominations is characterized by its own distinctives—public worship practices of the seven denominations vary from the casual—near freeform of the Baptists and Disciples to the structured liturgies of the Episcopalians and Lutherans.

With so reasonable a set of common characteristics, it is striking that so many of the members of their churches are leaving—opting for other churches with other priorities. Chapter eight is devoted to an extended discussion of the "whys" of membership departures. Surprisingly enough, some of the very qualities of the mainline churches in the fifties and sixties now may be found in abundance in evangelical churches. Hanna Rosin in her *New York Times* review of the Michlethwait and Wooldridge book *God Is Back* notes:

> Church became a place to form racial bonds, get dates, meet fellow moms isolated in suburbia, lose weight. Christian America spawned a parallel world of popular culture, with books and movies telling people how to live meaningful lives. The most popular, like Rick Warren's 'Purpose-driven Life' perfectly mirrored the can-do ethos of American success culture.[8]

A significant percentage of the members of the mainline churches left during the course of the last forty years. Of nearly equal importance, financial resources available to fund mainline ministries have declined, influence within American society has diminished, and confidence among the leaders of historic Protestantism is shaken.

Among the serious competitors of the mainline churches is fundamentalism.

Christian Fundamentalism

As the Enlightenment of the sixteenth century served to drive the Protestant Reformation, so the expansion of science in the nineteenth century was the unintended midwife at the birth of modern Christian fundamentalism. The Great Awakenings were responsible for moving American churches and American Christians from the sober intellectualism of Puritanism, which had dominated American religious thought for a century and a half, to personal religious *experience*. From mind to heart! Doctrine and thought counted for less, and the emotion engendered by the belief that being born again meant that one had experienced a personal relationship with Christ and was thereby saved from eternal punishment for sin.

Charles Darwin's *Origin of the Species* seemed a slap in the face of all Christians—those who held to doctrine, and those who relied on religious experience. Darwin told the world that the biblical account of creation was, in both the grand sweep of the story and its very details, wrong. There was, he held, an explanation for earth and all its features and creatures that was not dependent on divine action but upon a process that was knowable by humans.

At about the same time that Darwin's work became public, there arose in Germany a school of thought that said, in essence, Scripture is not what it seems to be or what the church had traditionally claimed it to be. The opening books of the Old Testament are the work of several authors (not Moses) working over a period of centuries, and the scholars held that by the exercise of careful methodology, it was possible to discern the source and the development of the stories and the strains of thought contained in those books. Known as the Graf-Welhausen hypothesis, the biblical scholars who propounded it treated the Bible as a human document which recounted humankind's search for knowledge of God—inspired, to be sure, but *not* dictated!

Preachers and laymen who had accepted the biblical story of creation as true and who trusted the Bible as a detailed and historically accurate record of God's dealings with humankind were moved, at their deepest levels, to discount and then to challenge both Darwin and the theory of evolution and the proponents of what came to be called "higher criticism" of the Judaeo-Christian scriptures.

Many churchmen refused to set aside their reliance on the Bible. They looked for ways to confound the Darwinian thesis and for techniques to discredit the biblical scholars ("not really Christians, you see"). The conservative preachers directed their energies to the saving of souls, to defeating Satan, to defending the infallibility of Scripture, to the imminent return of Christ to earth.

Other churchmen sought for ways to accommodate to the findings of both science and contemporary biblical scholarship while holding fast to their Christian faith. Often referred to as "modernists," these churchmen were characteristically to be found in the congregations of the historic Protestant denominations. Across the United States, local churches frequently became battlegrounds as the competing parties—modernists and fundamentalists—sought to prevail on matters theological and social. It was not uncommon for local churches to split as traditionalists walked away from friends and family in the name of theological purity.

As the nineteenth century drew to a close, a series of conferences known as the Niagara Bible Conferences emphasized, for Protestant Christians, the doctrines that were thought to comprise the core beliefs of Christians. Later, the Presbyterian Church, meeting in its 1910 General Assembly, building on the work of the Niagara Bible Conferences, identified what came to be known as the "five fundamentals" and declared that Presbyterians were to believe:

1. The inerrancy of the Scriptures.

2. The virgin birth and the deity of Jesus.

3. The doctrine of substitutionary atonement by God's grace through faith.

4. The bodily resurrection of Jesus and his bodily return to earth.

5. The authenticity of Christ's miracles.

In the second decade of the twentieth century, 1910–1915, conservative believers in the United States and Britain arranged for the publication of a series of books that gave explicit endorsement to and comment on what they considered the bedrock essentials of Christian theology. The series, which grew to a dozen volumes, was entitled, *The Fundamentals: A Testimony to the Truth*. Sixty-four American and British theologians penned the essays. More than a quarter of those essays assailed higher criticism. California millionaire Lyman Stewart, president of Union Oil Company, financed the project with a grant of a quarter of a million dollars to print and disseminate the essays. The essays were published, and some 3 million sets were distributed across the globe.[9]

Many of the most prominent Protestant clergy of the late nineteenth and early twentieth centuries were avid and compelling spokesmen for fundamentalism: Dwight Moody, Billy Sunday, William Riley (a backstage actor in the Scopes Trial), R. A. Torrey, James

Gay, J. Frank Norris, Cyrus Scofield, and J. Gresham Machen.

Christian fundamentalism may be defined by adherence to the five fundamentals, but it is often marked by behaviors expected of adherents.

- Attendance at movies or theater was/is seen as unacceptable[10] because of the subject matter and the lifestyles of actors and actresses.

- The drinking of alcoholic beverages was/is prohibited.

- Dancing was proscribed because of the touching of bodies and their movement.

- Sex outside of heterosexual marriage was prohibited, as is homosexual behavior, claimed by fundamentalists to be proscribed by Scripture.

Other behaviors are disallowed by some fundamentalist preachers and not by others—smoking tobacco, for example. The fact that American fundamentalism is strongest in the southern United States means that many of the churches of the Christian right are to be found in tobacco-growing states. In some of these states, cigarette or cigar smoking or the use of snuff may be allowed among male fundamentalist churchmen—rarely among women. Similarly, traditional patterns of dress and adornment are expected among some fundamentalist churches and ignored by others—especially those identified as counterculture Christians.

One of the propositions that, early on, was promoted by fundamentalist thinkers was that the believer was to be separate from those who were not Christian. That proposition was tweaked to mean that the Christians had to separate from those who held to different points of view about the Bible or the person and work of Christ. Drawing on the Holiness Code in the Old Testament (e.g., Leviticus 19-22) and some of the admonitions in the New Testament to be "separate" (e.g. Hebrews 7:26-27), strict fundamentalists avoid, insofar as possible, having anything do with other Christians who might not share their point of view or theological position. Exception to separatism exists for the purpose of conversion. Thus, Billy Graham, whose theological positions were largely, if not wholly, consistent with those of fundamentalist clergy, was scorned for cooperating in his crusades with churchmen who held to a different, more liberal theology. Academic institutions significantly to the right of center (Wheaton, Gordon, Biola, Talbot, for example) were and are not tolerated by strict fundamentalists. Thus, fundamentalists are understood by others as having to do only with those who think as they do.

Some positions that have little scriptural support are enthusiastically embraced by a majority of U.S. fundamentalists. Dispensationalism is one such position. First propounded by John Nelson Dailey, a Plymouth

Brethren minister in the early nineteenth century, dispensationalism held that all of God's promises to the nation of Israel would be literally fulfilled. Dispensationalism holds that the Bible teaches that there were seven distinct ways—dispensations—in which God has dealt or will deal with humans: paradise (i.e., Genesis), Noah and the Flood, Abraham, Israel, Gentiles, the Spirit, the millennium. Moreover, dispensationalists maintained that the church is distinct from Israel; God's promises to Israel and to the church are separate and, in God's time, both will be brought to pass, albeit not in the same way.

Many of the leading conservative churchmen of the nineteenth century became dispensationalists, including Dwight Moody and C. I. Scofield. The Moody Bible Institute, founded in 1889, propounded dispensationalist theology. The Scofield Reference Bible, with dispensationalist notes printed next to the biblical text, is to be found in virtually every fundamentalist church in the United States and, truth to tell, in most evangelical churches. It is, to this day, to be found in the hands of a startling percentage of churchmen, lay and ordained. Scofield wrote, "Each of the dispensations may be regarded as a new test of the material man, and each ends in judgment—marking his utter failure in every dispensation." Dallas Theological Seminary, the alma mater of many of the most conservative clergy in the nation, taught and promoted dispensational theology.

Dispensationalism is marked by a number of characteristics that make it especially appealing for fundamentalists to adopt: (a) the Bible is literally true, (b) an emphasis is placed on Bible prophecy, (c) a premillennial posture in reference to Christ's return is proclaimed (compared with material immediately following on "Rapture"), and (d) Christ's return is held to be likely at any moment.

A related theological position held by many fundamentalists is referred to as the Rapture. Again, with little support in Scripture (although often "proof-texted"), the Rapture propounds the view that any second, Christians will be taken up to meet Christ in the air. This event is said to precede seven years of tribulation which will end in the Battle of Armageddon and Christ's second coming to earth. The term *Rapture* appears in The Scofield Reference Bible, first published in 1909, although the idea of believers being "taken up" as an element of Christian eschatological thought had been around by that time for the better part of a century.

It is fair to say that a majority of conservative church members in the United States today hold to a point of view about the end-times that includes thoughts and visions of the Rapture. Lay members of fundamentalist and evangelical churches, and some outside those churches, give clear evidence of being intrigued by the idea of the Rapture. That fact takes public form in a variety of ways—from the displayed bumper sticker that reads, "Beware! This car will be empty at the Rapture"; to a score of popular movies, including *A Thief in the Night*; to Hal Lindsey's mega-seller, *The Late Great Planet Earth* (some estimate that sales reached 35 million copies); to Tim LaHaye's and Jerry B. Jenkins 1990s *Left Behind* series, with over 65 million books sold. (Three feature films have been made of books in the series.)

Associated with the Rapture are projections concerning the timing of Christ's return. Those projections raise questions about the projected tribulation; dispensationalists hold that it will come after the Rapture. They teach that Christ will return before a thousand years of peace (premillennialism), while others hold that it will follow the thousand years (postmillennialism). Some believe that Christ has already returned to earth (amillennialism).

The focus on and support of the state of Israel by fundamentalists is a concomitant of their eschatological views. Drawing on passages of Scripture which suggest that people will be drawn to Israel in the "last days" and that the temple in Jerusalem will be rebuilt as God prepares for the return of Jesus, Christian fundamentalists are among Israel's best friends. They encourage the US government to support Israel with financial aid and to provide arms. They side unhesitatingly with Israel in military actions against Palestinians and the Arab nations. There are Israeli protagonists from the smallest town in the nation to the halls of the U.S. Congress.

Perhaps the most extreme form of fundamentalist thought is called Dominionism. Dominionists are not large in number and are best seen as Israel-centric. Dominionists believe that God's laws are both specific and universal. They hold to the view that God's laws, as recorded in the Pentateuch, are binding on all people in all times. Despite the fact that those laws were given to the children of Israel in another age, Dominionists hold that they are applicable today.

Dominionists would convince the people of the United States of the need to match this nation's laws to those revealed and articulated in the Hebrew Scriptures. Once that has happened, freedom of religious choice will be eliminated. Those persons advocating or practicing beliefs other than Dominionism will be tried and, upon being found guilty, will be executed. Similarly, homosexuality and adultery will be criminalized, and those found guilty of engaging in such behavior or speaking on their behalf will be executed. Hard to believe, but these people, and this movement, really exist—albeit in small numbers. And it exists here in the United States.

In recent years, fundamentalists have adopted a political agenda. That agenda, shared for the most part with those who designate themselves "evangelicals," will be explored at greater length in the next chapter. The fundamentalist/evangelical political agenda focuses attention on:

- Halting the teaching of the theory of evolution in the public schools or, at minimum, promoting the teaching of creationism alongside (or in addition to) evolution.

- Eliminating all legislation that is perceived to allow for, or provide, special status or privileges for homosexuals, especially same-sex marriage.

- Overturning or otherwise making invalid the U.S. Supreme Court decision (*Roe v. Wade*) allowing abortion.

- Assigning a very specific role to women— e.g., the married woman must defer to her husband, the female Christian must not be ordained, etc.

A wide variety of other related and unrelated political positions are attached to fundamentalism: demanding lower taxes, denying the evidence of global climate change, opposing stem cell research, etc. The effect of fundamentalism's political agenda has been the development of an informal but powerful linkage of Christian fundamentalism to the Republican Party; a second effect has been to drive Republican Party positions hard to the right and to eliminate or eviscerate that party's moderate wing.

Fundamentalist Christians are to be found in independent churches, in churches which proclaim themselves nondenominational, in churches which are affiliated with organizations created specifically for them (e.g., the Calvary Church movement), and in some churches which remain within a mainline denomination. But by every measure, the largest ecclesiastical organization which embraces the fundamentalist perspective is the Southern Baptist Convention.

Until the late 1950s, the Southern Baptist Convention, while clearly conservative[11], was nonetheless "home" to some institutions and scholars who were accepting of methodologies that led to biblical or theological conclusions that fundamentalists' charge were too moderate, liberal, or even modernist.

When Ralph Elliott's *The Message of Genesis* was released in 1961, a storm of controversy followed in churches of the Southern Baptist Convention. Elliott was professor of Old Testament at one of the SBC schools, Midwestern Baptist Theological Seminary in Kansas City, and his use of historical/critical methodology led him to conclude that the early chapters in Genesis were mythological in nature. In state conventions and SBC publications, Elliott's work was harshly criticized. The next year, one of Elliott's most prominent critics, the pastor of First Baptist Church in Houston, the Reverend K. O. White, was elected president of the Southern Baptist Convention in large measure because of his outrage at Elliott's book and his organized efforts to have the book banned and Elliott fired. Thus began a concerted, organized effort by fundamentalists to "take over" the Southern Baptist Convention, its schools, and other manifestations of institutional life.[12] (Supporters of the effort reject the term *fundamentalist takeover* and refer to the effort as the *Conservative Resurgence*).

By the 1970 Convention of the Southern Baptists, the encounter between moderates and fundamentalists had deteriorated to a near-brawl. The 1970s became the decade in which Southern Baptists on the theological right mounted their strategy to take over the SBC and to eliminate all influences that might be perceived as liberal. Key to the strategy was the power of the president of the Southern Baptist Convention to appoint members to the committees of the denomination. The term of office for these positions was five years, renewable once. The fundamentalist strategists concluded that were they to elect one of their own as president *for each of the next ten years*, they would be able, by reason of presidential appointees, to control the Southern Baptist Convention in perpetuity. Beginning with the election of the Reverend Adrian Rogers of Memphis in 1979 and continuing to today, the right wing of the SBC has elected the presidents and, thus, exerted total control over the denomination.

The plan by fundamentalists to control the Southern Baptist Convention and its success in doing so has led to a reaction. In 1987, the Alliance of Baptists was formed by a number of the more liberal Baptist churches. The group is small (about 200-member churches) and is generally comfortable with theological and social positions that are characteristic of those held by the churches in mainstream Protestantism.

In 1990, the Cooperative Baptist Fellowship (CBF) was created out of the desire to position member churches more clearly in the mainstream of American religious life and thought. CBF churches do not hold to the separatism of classic fundamentalism and thought. Considerably larger than the Alliance of Baptists, the CBF numbers nearly 2,000 churches, and it is fair to say that few in other denominations would define CBF churches or leaders as "liberal."

Interestingly, some new entities have come into being to stand for and promote historic Baptist principles: Baptist Women in Ministry, Smith & Helwys Publishers, Associated Baptist Press, and a number of Baptist educational institutions.

Despite these efforts to maintain a more open, less rigid posture on matters theological, biblical, and social, the fact is that the Southern Baptists are "riding high." Christians from other parts of the country report that when job or family responsibilities cause them to move to a southern town or city, they are overwhelmed by the pervasive power of the local Southern Baptist churches. A seatmate on a recent flight said to me, "It is almost as though I had no choice about which church I would attend. My neighbors, my colleagues, my golfing buddies were all Baptists, and they simply assumed I would be a Baptist too and share their beliefs and political points of view."

Claiming 16,270,315 members (2007) in 44,000 churches, the SBC is the largest Protestant denomination in the United States and is more than twice the size of the next largest, the United Methodist Church.

The name, Southern Baptist Convention, has become a misnomer. Although it implies a geographic region for its operations and, indeed, can trace its origins to the run up to the Civil War when the Baptists in the Old South severed or severely limited their relations with their Baptist brethren in the North, the Southern Baptist Convention is organized and operational in all fifty states. As recently as the 1940s, the expansion of the SBC in the north, east, and west was a debatable proposition, not an aggressive policy. In fact, there existed some agreements between Northern Baptists and Southern Baptists to stay out of each other's way. Those agreements were set aside as early as 1950, as the Southern Baptists flooded the nation with ministers and missionaries.

Fundamentalism then may be defined as representing theological, social, and political views on the far right. Although persons holding fundamentalist views are to be found in independent churches and in some mainline churches, their largest and most powerful institutional base is in the Southern Baptist churches. Not all conservative Christians may be identified as fundamentalists; a strong and vital movement identified as "evangelical" characterizes much of the Christian right.

The Evangelicals/
Neo-Evangelicals

It is important to recognize that virtually all Protestant churches in North America were conservative/orthodox in matters theological until virtually the end of the eighteenth century. The faithful, lay and ordained alike, held to the historic creeds and trusted in the infallibility of Scripture.

The First and Second Great Awakenings (eighteenth and nineteenth centuries) propelled an experiential, emotion-driven Protestantism that served to validate traditional Christianity. Toward the end of the eighteenth century, in response to ideas promulgated by some European thinkers and the growing acceptance of the findings of science, a few American Christians began to question traditional formulations of their faith. Deism and its absent watchmaker was one form the questioning took; Unitarianism was another.

What is telling, however, when looking at this phenomenon from the vantage of time, is that the prevailing theology, values, and social thought held. In 1900, the messages preached in a vast majority of the pulpits of all the denominations in the United States were similar to what they had been a hundred years earlier.

The theology resident behind the message proclaimed from the pulpits in fundamentalist and evangelical churches today is remarkably similar to that which British and American preachers were propounding in, say, 1750. Those theological positions were orthodox in the sense that they drew on and were representative of historic Christian thinking;[13] they were evangelical in a Pauline or Lutheran sense, in that they proclaimed the good news of Christ crucified, Christ risen, salvation by grace through faith.

It was not until the middle of the nineteenth century that Protestant Christianity in the United States began to separate into many contending factions: on the one hand were those who were deeply opposed to the findings or theories of modern science, relying for validation on their personal experience with Christ, and on the other were those who sought for ways to accommodate science while remaining unashamedly Christian. The contentiousness flowing from the differences produced an angst and distrust within American Protestantism that continues to this day.

Sometime around the outset of World War II, perhaps a bit earlier, fundamentalists who had so proudly borne that designation in the years following the publication of *A Testimony to Truth* began to display a measure of reticence, to use that term as a self-descriptor. The larger society, those within and without the church, tended to judge fundamentalists as "back-woodsy," anti-intellectual, uneducated, and uninformed. The phrase *fighting fundamentalists* was used by many Christians, and it had a decidedly negative connotation because of the role fundamentalists played in splitting churches and getting ministers fired. Even convinced fundamentalists reacted negatively to the ways in which they were viewed. Kenneth Kantzer, in *The Fundamentalist—Evangelical Split* reported that the term *fundamentalist* had become "an embarrassment instead of a badge of honor."

The term *conservative* or *conservative evangelical* began to be seen with greater regularity in fundamentalist literature. By the late 1970s, even the Southern Baptist fundamentalists who had been so successful in taking over the SBC were eschewing the term *fundamentalist takeover* to describe their efforts and their successes; they preferred and promoted the usage of *Conservative Resurgence*.

Movements, whether religious or political or social/cultural, rarely have margins that are absolutely crisp and clean. Who is a fundamentalist and who an evangelical were questions difficult to decide. They remain so. One factor on which such a determination could be made was that fundamentalists held to separation, or separatism, as a biblical imperative—"don't fraternize with the enemy." There were some who shared many, or all, of the theological positions enunciated in the "five fundamentals" but who found themselves uncomfortable with the idea that they could have nothing to do with persons who claimed the name of Christ but held to a somewhat different set of theological propositions. Others, while examining higher criticism of Scripture for ways to undermine its findings, became convinced by those findings or appreciative of some of its insights and stopped calling themselves fundamentalists. Not all conservative evangelicals were comfortable with or accepting of dispensationalism, which had won most fundamentalists and many who called themselves evangelicals.

Conservative, those folks might be, and evangelical, they surely were, but fundamentalist, as a designation, no longer fit. This was the case, even though they might share the fundamentalists' political agenda—i.e., no to abortion, no to homosexual marriage, no to the teaching of evolution, no to ordaining women, etc. And this was true, even though an evangelical might agree with and promote the behavioral demands of the fundamentalists: don't dance, don't go to movies or the theater, don't consume alcoholic beverages, don't ever engage in any form of sexual behavior outside of marriage.

It can be argued that the decision by Billy Graham to involve Christians who were not fundamentalists in his crusades was the most important factor in leading large numbers of evangelical Christians to split off from, or give up on, what might be called "classic fundamentalism." Graham might have been the most prominent conservative clergyman to break ranks with fundamentalism—and remember, he agreed in most respects with their theology. He was not the only one. As early as the 1920s, J. Gresham Machen denounced dispensationalism. Carl Henry was to adopt a critical posture toward separatism; John MacArthur, Sr., and Jr. both repudiated "biblical separation."

In 1947, the Reverend Harold John Ockenga, pastor of the famous Park Street Congregational Church in Boston, spoke at a conference in Pasadena, California, in which he coined the term *neo-evangelical*. Ockenga's church claimed the name *congregational*, which was also the designation claimed by the most liberal of the mainline denominations. Ockenga himself, whose credentials as a member of the Christian right were clear, argued that Christians ought to engage constructively those whose beliefs were different from their own. It was his position that if one wanted to win a person to the conservative evangelical agenda, one had to meet that person. For Ockenga, separation was out the door; persuasion was in.

In the decade following Ockenga's speech, *Christianity Today* was founded (1956) as an answer to *The Christian Century*, the highly regarded journal of liberal Christian thought.[14] With Carl F. H. Henry, a leading evangelical as editor, *Christianity Today* soon built a solid subscription base and gave voice—more often than not, thoughtful voice—to the views of evangelical clergy and the faculties of evangelical educational institutions.

At about the same time, Fuller Theological Seminary was founded in Pasadena, California, by Charles

E. Fuller, a popular radio preacher of the 1930s and 40s. Fuller's network broadcasts had emanated every Sunday from the Long Beach, California, Municipal Auditorium. He is warmly remembered for his folksy on-air conversations with his wife for his down-to-earth albeit ultra conservative, sermons, and for the gospel ditty "Heavenly Sunshine." Harold John Ockenga became president of Fuller Seminary and served both his Boston church and the Pasadena seminary for some years.

The evangelical cause has been well-served by both *Christianity Today*, whose subscribers now (2009) number 145,000,[15] and Fuller Seminary, which claims 5,000 students enrolled in its graduate and professional degree programs (2009). There are, of course, many other evangelical publications and a solid group of evangelical colleges and seminaries. Campus Crusade, Youth for Christ, Focus on the Family all may be seen as parts of the institutional infrastructure serving and buttressing modern-day evangelicalism. The National Association of Evangelicals, founded in 1942, seeks to be and, indeed, has positioned itself as the national voice of evangelicals in the United States.

The National Association of Evangelicals is comprised of some sixty denominations with nearly 45,000 churches, colleges, mission organizations, individual churches, and para-church organizations. The statement of faith of the organization, though clearly inspired by the "five fundamentals," is more expansive and, some would say, more nuanced and sophisticated:

- "We believe the Bible to be the inspired, the only infallible, authoritative Word of God.

- We believe that there is one God, eternally existent in three persons: Father, Son, and Holy Spirit.

- We believe in the deity of our Lord Jesus Christ, in His virgin birth, in His sinless life, in His miracles, in His vicarious and atoning death through His shed blood, in His bodily resurrection, in His ascension to the right hand of the Father, and in His personal return in power and glory.

- We believe that for the salvation of lost and sinful people, regeneration by the Holy Spirit is absolutely essential.

- We believe in the present ministry of the Holy Spirit by whose indwelling the Christian is enabled to live a godly life.

- We believe in the resurrection of both the saved and the lost; they that are saved unto the resurrection of life, and they that are lost unto the resurrection of damnation.

- We believe in the spiritual unity of believers in our Lord Jesus Christ."

Fundamentalists and evangelicals alike have often been criticized for ignoring the challenges and problems of contemporary society. The National Association of Evangelicals, following a study lasting several years, adopted a statement called "For the Health of the Nation: An Evangelical Call to Civic Responsibility." The full statement is informed by NAE's seven principles that focus on political engagement:

1. "We work to protect religious freedom and liberty of conscience.

2. We work to nurture family life and protect children.

3. We seek to protect the sanctity of human life and to safeguard its nature.

4. We seek justice and compassion for the poor and vulnerable.

5. We work to protect human rights.

6. We seek peace and work to restrain violence.

7. We labor to protect God's creation."[16]

Evangelicals today are to be found as conservative members of churches of mainline denominations, as well as in churches described as nondenominational, independent, Baptist, Calvary, or Bible churches.

Although the statistics may seem imprecise, there is some agreement that evangelicals in the United States today number in excess of 35 percent of the population.[17]

This compares with Catholics in the United States, who represent about 25 percent of the population.

It is noteworthy that among African American church members, a majority are evangelicals. Significantly, African American evangelicals seem not to share the political agenda (cf. p. 42) of white evangelicals but do embrace such marks of evangelicalism as the importance of the conversion and the born-again experience. The term *born again* is frequently used to identify persons of the evangelical persuasion; it refers to a specific personal religious experience that marks the beginning of new life in Christ.

It is important to note that mainline Protestants and evangelicals have much in common. The roots of both are deep in American life; they are likely to be members of the same PTAs, to go to the polls with regularity, to support community projects like the United Way and the local hospital, to work at the same kinds of jobs. Their differences sharpen on such matters as the teachings of evolution, the rights of homosexuals, the responses to the termination of pregnancy, the claims made for the Bible, and for what and for whom they vote.

The structure and organization of life in their respective local churches is likely to be similar, if not identical—democracy prevails with lay members exerting significant influence if not total control; congregational or parish business is financed by voluntary gifts and pledges.

Services of worship in mainline and evangelical churches, on the surface, feel different; even casual analysis will reveal, however, their deep similarities—both have grown from the Service of the Word in the early church, even as that service evolved from the Synagogue Service of Hellenistic Judaism. In both mainline and evangelical services of worship hymns, prayers, Scripture readings all preface an instructional homily or sermon. It is true that evangelical services of worship are likely to be significantly more informal than those in a mainline church. Hymns are different much of the time with mainline hymnody drawing extensively on the music of the Reformation and the classical traditions, while the evangelical churches will feature music that tends to have roots that are much more recent. Instrumentation differs: organs and pianos for the mainline; electronic keyboards, guitars, and drums for the evangelicals.

Both include baptism and the Lord's Supper in worship but with marked differences: among evangelicals, believer's baptism by immersion and bread with grape juice in the pews for the Lord's Supper. Most, not all, of the mainline churches practice infant baptism and utilize bread and wine—often at the altar—in celebration of the Eucharist. In short, the worship differences are defined on the traditional/contemporary continuum. Prayers in mainline churches are likely to be carefully, even artfully, composed and taken from, or inspired by, books of worship. Prayers in evangelical churches are, most frequently, extemporaneous-conversational rather than artful. It is the informal contemporaneity of modern evangelicalism, along with its firm stands on the infallibility of Scripture and the promise of salvation, that has proved to be so compelling for many Christians.

There is no denying the dynamic of modern evangelicalism. Persons little concerned with theological propositions have demonstrated that the small groups, the informality, the clear and crisp answers to vexing questions which are characteristic of the evangelical churches are powerful attractions. Some denominations which share some characteristics with the evangelicals have a powerful and growing presence in North and South America, Asia, and Africa.

Pentecostalists and Charismatics

Claiming as many as 200 million adherents worldwide,[18] with more than 20 million in the United States, Pentecostalism is a movement within Protestant Christianity that demands, by virtue of numbers alone, to be taken seriously. With an institutional history of little more than one hundred years, Pentecostalism is arguably the most rapidly growing group in Christendom, with remarkable strength in South America, Africa, and Asia.

Few movements spring full-blown from nothing, and so it is with Pentecostalism. The movement may claim, legitimately, to inherit the history described in Acts 2 when the Holy Spirit descended on Peter and other followers of Jesus on Pentecost. *Pentecost* is the Greek term for the Jewish Feast of Weeks; the gathering in Jerusalem, reported in Acts, took place shortly after Jesus's ascension, and the events associated with it are often referred to as the birth of the Christian Church.

One of the notable events occurring on the day of Pentecost was that Jesus's followers spoke in foreign tongues and were thus enabled to make converts of men and women from other nations. The New Testament text has the term *tongues*, referring to speech in languages other than Hebrew or Aramaic, which the disciples were said to be enabled to do. The term *tongues* is, today, utilized most often to refer to largely unintelligible sounds, syllables, apparent words, and sentences. The technical term is *glossolalia* and is sometimes a mark of religious ecstasy.

To some degree or other, speaking in tongues in an ecstatic state was doubtlessly practiced in some quarters through the long years of Christian history, though records of such are slim.

In the nineteenth century, a movement that came to be called the Holiness Movement arose in the United States. Largely, if not totally, dependent on John Wesley's theology of sanctification and perfection, the Holiness Movement taught that humankind is saved by God's grace through faith *and* after being reborn, he/she may be sanctified by a second work of grace through the Holy Spirit. *Sanctification* is (or may be) accompanied by visible signs, one of which is speaking in tongues. It is appropriate to see the Holiness Movement as having grown and developed from Methodism but came to engage persons of other denominational affiliations.[19]

When one takes note of the First and Second Great Awakenings (eighteenth and nineteenth centuries) and their emphasis on religious experience and personal conversion, it is not surprising that in 1836, a series of meetings promoting holiness and personal perfection commenced in New York City under the leadership of two Methodist women, Sarah Lankford and Phoebe Palmer. Their Tuesday meetings grew in attendance and prominence. The involvement of women in these meetings and in the subsequent development of the Holiness Movement is evident in the leadership of women today in churches of denominations associated with, or growing out of, holiness.

It was not long before men—many of them prominent Christian leaders—identified themselves with the Holiness Movement.

In the last third of the nineteenth century, the movement had grown so that Holiness Camp Meetings were held in the eastern United States, which attracted thousands of participants. Experiences in these meetings were said to be so powerful spiritually that supporters came to identify them with the events which took place on the first Christian Pentecost.

These activities and the leadership growing from them led to the founding of churches which embraced Christian Holiness and the gathering of such churches into partnerships/associations or denominations committed to sanctification and perfection while practicing the gifts growing from sanctification (tongues, interpretation of tongues, prophecy, healing). Among those embracing the Holiness Movement were African American men and women. And while much of the early momentum for Holiness came from the Christian men and women on the East Coast of the United States, the movement spread rapidly, via revival meetings, to the Midwestern and southern United States.

As the nineteenth century drew to a close, speculation about the return of Jesus on or about the year 1900 became rampant. Intense religious feelings were common across the spectrum of Protestant Christianity.

Charles Parham, president of Bethel Bible College in Topeka, Kansas, and a Holiness preacher, led a revival meeting in Topeka. One of those attending on a seminal date, January 1, 1900, Agnes Ozman, spoke fluently in a number of languages she reported that she had never previously known or studied. This event is thought by some to be the founding of the modern Pentecostal movement. It is noteworthy that several others during their attendance at the revival, including Parham himself, received the gift of tongues.

One of Parham's African American students, William Seymour, had founded a church in his home in Los Angeles, California. On April 9, 1906, during a service of worship, Seymour's landlord and a coworker, Edward Lee and Jennie Moore respectively, experienced the gift of tongues. As word of that remarkable event got out, attendance in the little home church grew rapidly and to such an extent that Seymour's home was no longer adequate. A former African Methodist Episcopal Church at 312 Azusa Street was rented and thus began the famous Azusa Street revival. For over three years, the "Apostolic Faith Mission" held three services a day, seven days a week. Thousands received the gift of tongues.

From Los Angeles, the Pentecostal movement spread throughout California and into the northwest and, soon, around the world. One of the marks of the Pentecostalism of the early twentieth century was its color blindness; blacks and whites worshiped together. Black and white ministers led integrated churches.

Until World War I, the Pentecostal movement was to be found primarily in Holiness churches. Strains developed, however, between those who had practiced sanctification and perfection in Holiness churches for many years and those who had come later via the Azusa Street movement. And, sad to note, the relationship which had existed between and among blacks and whites led to the founding of segregated Pentecostal churches which did not have direct ties to Holiness.

Some Holiness churches, associations, even denominations moved over to the institutions of Pentecostalism. Others retained, to this day, their own historic identity. Pentecostalism took institutional form in a number of denominations, including the Church of God in Christ (5.5 million plus members), the Church of God (Cleveland, Tennessee), the Assemblies of God (2.5 million members), the International Church of the Foursquare Gospel, Pentecostal Church of God, Pentecostal Assemblies of the World, United Pentecostal Church International, and many others.

In doctrine, most of the Pentecostal groups may be said to hold orthodox views on the classic elements of the Christian story: the Trinity, virgin birth, the miracles, atonement, return of Christ. They believe in the literal word of the Bible. Two groups within the movement—United Pentecostal Church International and Pentecostal Assemblies of the World—are referred to as *Oneness Pentecostals*. They believe that baptism should be done in the name of Jesus alone and that the traditional concept of the Trinity is wrong (their argument is not unlike that to which the Eastern Christians held following the Council of Chalcedon).

Given the racial integration of the churches of Pentecostalism in the early years of the movement, it is not surprising that services of worship in Pentecostal churches bear similarities to services in historic Black churches—i.e., informal with uninhibited verbal contributions from members of the congregation: "Amen!" "That's right!" "Praise God!" Foot washing is a common practice and is seen as an act of humility. Speaking in tongues is characteristic and seen as a mark of sanctification and of commitment to personal perfection.

Highly successful in appealing to the poor and the dispossessed throughout the world, mainline Christians nonetheless make a serious mistake in believing that only those from the underclass are drawn to Pentecostalism. In fact, the movement has made remarkable inroads in appealing to the middle class in the United States, Canada, and Western Europe.

Pentecostalists have been successful in influencing the charismatic movement—a movement within mainline churches and churches of other denominations. The term *charismatic* comes from the Greek *charis* (grace or gift) and is used in this context to describe Christians who hold that the gifts of the Holy Spirit (glossalalia, prophecy, healing, etc.) are available today.

David du Plessis, a Pentecostal minister, is considered to be one of the major influences in the birth and growth of the modern charismatic movement. He is noteworthy for his relationships with the Roman Catholic Church and as a Pentecostal observer at Vatican Council II. The charismatic movement is alive and well in contemporary Catholicism, especially in the Far East. It has been reported that the pastor of Pope John Paul II was a charismatic priest.

The other name associated with the founding of the charismatic movement is the Reverend Dennis Bennett. Rector of St. Mark's Episcopal Church in Van Nuys, California, Bennett announced to his congregation in 1960 that he had received the outpouring of the Holy Spirit. From a base in Vancouver, Canada, Bennett's efforts are credited with having an influence on Lutheran, Roman Catholic, and Orthodox churches, as well as his own Episcopal church.

Charismatic Christians—that is, those who believe they have received one of another of the gifts of the Holy Spirit—tended to remain in the churches of their own denominations. I remember being told quietly and humbly by a stalwart Episcopalian lady one Sunday, "I have the gift." Since the late 1980s, many of the charismatics have left the churches in which they have held their memberships to join Pentecostal churches or churches and denominations of their own creation where worship services can make room for expressions of the gifts of the Holy Spirit.

While the charismatic movement is characteristically seen as a renewal movement (cf. The Vineyard Movement), some United States Christians are profoundly critical of it—notably those in Reformed Church circles and some Southern Baptist leaders and institutions. Their inclusion in this chapter is due to the fact that Pentecostalists often identify with evangelicals. And it is a fact that Pentecostalists share most of their beliefs with evangelical Christians. In short, Pentecostalists hold to biblical inerrancy and the need for individual persons to be born again by faith in Jesus. For Pentecostalists the baptism of the Holy Spirit, if it occurs in a given Christian, most often typically follows the salvation or born-again experience.

Pentecostalists are widely known for including the speaking in tongues (glossolalia) as a legitimate part of the Christian's experience although most believe that the Holy Spirit manifests additional or other gifts including interpretation of tongues, healing, prophecy, words of wisdom, etc.

Pentecostalists are Arminian,[20] as opposed to Calvinist, in theology. Some Pentecostalists do not hold to classic Trinitarianism, preferring to describe God as having three manifestations.

While the charismatic movement owes much to Pentecostalism, it is clear that the lifestyles of the groups differ significantly. Some commentators would identify Pentecostalists as naïve and charismatics as sophisticated—a rough cut at showing the distinctives but perhaps suggestive of differing lifestyles.

The number of Charismatics worldwide is impossible to assert with any degree of accuracy, but some have claimed, in their enthusiasm, that they are now equal in number to Pentecostalists.

Pentecostalists and Charismatics are markedly similar to evangelicals in thought and institutional culture. They bring something more—viz., ecstasy—to their faith practices. There are some contemporary Christians who believe that they know some things about the Christian message that others—including mainline churchmen or women, fundamentalists or evangelicals—don't know. Their "secret" knowledge is a major strength in winning converts.

Modern-Day Gnostics

Those who have, in the last forty years, been the big winners in making converts of members of the mainline churches, who have, in fact, sparked the defections, are clearly the fundamentalists and evangelicals. They, and the churches they represent, are not, however, the only ones who have been contending for the support of Episcopalians and Presbyterians and the others who have heretofore held membership in one of the mainline churches.

The adherents to movements, labeled here as modern-day Gnostics, have been aggressive missionaries who are certain of the truth of their movements. Before looking in specific terms at portions of some of the more prominent churches that may be defined as Gnostic, it is appropriate to ask: what is Gnosticism, and do the contemporary movements designated Gnostic lay claim to holding truth(s) that mainstream Protestantism rejects?

Gnosticism refers to a mix of philosophical/religious sects, some of which pre-dated Christianity and others of which flourished during the early history of the church. The Greek word *gnosis* means knowledge, and it was characteristic of the Gnostic sects that adherents believed they were in possession of knowledge that was unknown to others. That knowledge could be known only to initiates of the specific sect. In that sense, Gnostics may be seen as having secret knowledge. The Gnostics of two thousand years ago held that they received personal revelations of God and his truths.

There were many permutations of Christian Gnosticism. In recent years, a variety of manuscripts have been found in the Middle East representing the views of one or another of the early Christian Gnostic sects.[21] In 2006, one of those manuscripts, *The Gospel of Judas*, was published, accompanied by the breathless noise of the modern publicity machine.

The ensuing furor was characteristic of Gnosticism in that *The Gospel of Judas* articulated a position that was skewed from that held by the main body of Christian thought, viz. that Judas's "betrayal" of Jesus was not betrayal at all but an action of Judas in which he fulfilled the role to which he had been assigned by Jesus and was an act intended to precipitate the kingdom of God. *The Gospel of Judas* and the interpretation of Judas's actions were, and are, classic Gnosticism: it purported to be based on knowledge that others did not possess. The problem with the furor caused by the publication of *The Gospel of Judas* is that some normative Christians have posited such a rationale or motive for Judas's actions since the earliest days of the church. *The Gospel of Judas* is not and was not secret at all.

Even though the manuscript is a relatively recent find, early Christians knew it existed and made reference to it. The public furor engendered by *The Gospel of Judas* has stirred up interest in some of the other apocryphal/Gnostic writings from the early Christian centuries: *The Gospel of Peter*, *The Gospel of Mary*, etc. There are some who would attribute greater credence to them than to the books of the Canon. There seems to be no end of persons who argue that the decisions regarding the writings sanctioned for inclusion in the Canon of the New Testament were political decisions that did not necessarily represent the gospel as delivered by Jesus or the will of God. "How do we know," they insist, "that the words purported to have come from Jesus in Matthew really were his words? Why not the words assigned to Jesus in Judas, for example?"

Altogether apart from the faith of the committed churchman that God acts through the decisions and actions of His people—i.e., the church—and may thereby be accorded a measure of respect, there is the fact that the early Christians depended on the message delivered them by the apostles and their successors. The apostles were with Jesus. They were chosen by Jesus to spread his message. All messages purporting to come from Jesus must have passed through his apostles. "We believe in one holy catholic and apostolic Church."[22]

Throughout the ages there have been movements and churches and messages that claim to be faithful to the gospel—only their gospel differs in significant ways from the apostolic gospel. And as it has been throughout the ages, so it is today: there are many modern-day movements that may appropriately be labeled *Gnostic*. We are going to look at the positions taken by three of them, all of which engage in aggressive proselytizing. The success of their efforts varies from time to time and movement to movement, but the intensity of their efforts is not diminished. The three are: The Church of Jesus Christ of Latter-day Saints (Mormon), Jehovah's Witnesses, and the Seventh-day Adventist Church.

The Church of Jesus Christ of Latter-day Saints

The Church of Jesus Christ of Latter-day Saints can trace its origins to upper New York State in the third decade of the nineteenth century. The region was known as the Burned-Over District after the impact on its inhabitants by the Second Great Awakening.

Joseph Smith, Jr., a farm boy in Palmyra, New York, claimed to have become so troubled by the discord in the churches around him that he retired to the woods to seek wisdom from God. He was visited there by the Father and the Son, who instructed him to set himself apart from the contending denominations for a special task he was to be given.

After having been tested and receiving additional revelations, Joseph was visited by the angel Moroni, who guided him to buried golden plates that told the story of the Nephites and Lamanites, descendants of the lost tribes of Israel. According to the plates, the two groups lived in North America and had been visited by Christ there after his resurrection. The Lamanites had become apostate and engaged in a fearsome battle with the Nephites. In the battle, all of the Nephites save only Mormon and his son, Moroni, were killed.

The golden plates, Smith said, had been written in Reformed Egyptian hieroglyphics, which he had been enabled to translate using a special translating stone. Ultimately, both the golden plates and the stone were returned to the angels, but *The Book of Mormon* reporting the revelations which Smith had translated into English was published in 1830 in Palmyra, New York.

In that same year, the twenty-four-year-old Joseph Smith and five friends founded the Church of Christ that later came to be known as the Church of Latter-day Saints and finally was named the Church of Jesus Christ of Latter-day Saints.

The Book of Mormon drew special attention, for it provided definitive answers to questions that troubled the churches and churchmen of the time—questions covering everything from infant baptism to the fall of man and most issues in between. *The Book of Mormon* also set forth the view that America was the "promised land"—a view that added to the general excitement the publication engendered.

It was held that Smith and his assistant, Oliver Cowdery, were ordained by John the Baptist, who appeared before them. As the new church organized, members were told to "give heed unto all his (Smith's) words and commandments" as though they came directly from the mouth of God.

Mormon history is well-known; Smith and his followers, in time, set forth on a journey that led them from New York through Ohio to Missouri and Illinois. It was in Illinois that the church's founder was brutally murdered in 1844. In 1843, Smith claimed to receive a revelation initiating polygamy—this was in spite of the monogamy previously required of members in *The Book of Mormon*. Smith was succeeded as leader of the church by Brigham Young, who proved to be a leader of rare ability. Young organized and led the cross-country trek that would eventually take his people to the Great Salt Lake in the region that was to become the state of Utah.

During his lifetime, Joseph Smith was credited with writing, among other things, *Doctrines and Covenants* and *Pearl of Great Price*, the contents both of which were said to have been revealed to him. The Church of Jesus Christ of Latter-day Saints claimed three sources of revelation: the Bible, the *Book of Mormon*, and the other books of Joseph Smith containing and commenting on the direct revelations received from God. While the Bible is referenced with great regularity in Mormon practice, it appears to take an inferior position to *The Book of Mormon* and *Doctrines and Covenants*.

It is important to contemporary Mormons to hold that they are Christians. They point out that the very name of their church puts Jesus Christ front and center. Despite that insistence, the doctrines of the church are far from orthodox Christianity. The Church of Jesus Christ of Latter-day Saints holds to a plurality of gods, to a mother goddess, to the potential for "good" Mormons to become gods. Indeed, their teachings go so far as to proclaim that God was, at one time, a man on a distant planet.

Of the Trinity, LDS doctrine maintains that there are three gods, that God the Father is married, and with his wife they have "spirit children." Jesus and Satan are said to be spirit brothers; the Holy Ghost is a man. Mormons believe in, and engage in, a practice known as celestial marriage—a marriage that is intended to last beyond death and through eternity. According to LDS doctrine, earthly couples may seek to have their marriages "sealed" by an official in a Mormon Temple. They are enjoined to follow Jesus Christ and to have their sealing confirmed by God through His Spirit.

Members of the Church of Jesus Christ of Latter-day Saints endorse and engage in the practice of baptism for the dead.[23] Believing that baptism is a requisite for entry into the kingdom of God, a living person is immersed in water on behalf of a deceased person and baptized according to the Trinitarian formula. Baptisms for the dead must take place in a Mormon Temple—of which there are approximately seventy in the world with perhaps two dozen more announced or currently under construction. Members are diligent in researching persons who are deceased and baptizing them by proxy so that they might enter God's kingdom.

Sunday services in LDS meeting houses are lengthy—typically three hours or more long. The first hour finds men and women separated: Men attend what is known as a priesthood meeting in which the business of the local ward of the church is conducted, while women participate in a meeting of the Relief Society, devoted primarily to homemaking, child rearing, charity works, and the like. The second hour is given to Sunday school; classes are held for all ages, young and old, and those classes, led for the most part by fellow members, focus on Mormon doctrines and practices. The third hour is the sacrament meeting which consists of readings, hymns, homilies and testimonies, and the celebration of the sacrament. The sacrament consists of bread and water.

The Church of Jesus Christ of Latter-day Saints is a laymen's and women's movement. There is no professional clergy. Services are led by members of the ward (local church), including baptisms, confirmations, marriages, funerals, etc. Even as one ascends the organizational ladder—officers are lay people set apart for specific duties. While there are no Mormon seminaries in the Catholic or Protestant sense, instruction for lay leaders comes from the church hierarchy headquartered in Salt Lake City and is thorough, detailed, and challenging.

LDS members are encouraged to lay away food stuffs and other essentials for an anticipated future time of famine or reduced accessibility to necessities.

Members of the Church of Jesus Christ of Latter-day Saints are diligent in engaging in efforts to retain the loyalty of their youth. Males, from an early age, are members of age-appropriate Boy Scouts of America troops. Girls are served through the LDS Young Women's programs. Dances, parties, picnics, and outdoor camping experiences are typical of activities designed for and provided to Mormon youth, male and female.

Mormonism has always been marked by its strong commitment to missions. From the very beginning, members have diligently sought to win converts. By 1870, a mere forty years after its founding, the church is said to have numbered 140,000 members. Proselytizing today focuses on the efforts of young men and women[24] who commit two years of their lives to their Mormon mission. They may be found in population centers throughout the world—fresh faced, well scrubbed, and nicely dressed—moving door to door to spread the Mormon message. By reason of their missionary zeal, many LDS members are convinced their faith will ultimately become dominant throughout the world, and they report, enthusiastically, astonishing growth for their church. At this writing (2010), they claim 13 million members worldwide and 5,873,408 in the United States. Over three-fourths of their US membership is in the West. There is reason to have some question about their membership numbers:

reportedly, there is a church sanctioned practice in which defections from Mormonism are not counted—i.e., not subtracted from the membership rolls.

The Pew Forum on Religion and Public Life reports that Mormon membership is young (the largest cohort is in the thirty to forty-nine age range) and overwhelmingly white (over 80 percent). It also reports that LDS members are relatively well-off (16 percent have annual incomes of $100,000 or more).

Jehovah's Witnesses

Members of this group are conspicuous and diligent in their efforts to share their vision of salvation and win converts to their movement. Their founder, Charles Taze Russell, was the owner of a men's clothing store and a lay member of a congregational church in Pennsylvania in the years following the Civil War. Russell founded a Bible study group that, years later, evolved into Jehovah's Witnesses. His teachings were clearly influenced by the Millerites/Adventists whose efforts preceded his own by some thirty years.

Key to an understanding of the Jehovah's Witnesses is their belief that they are living in the last days. In a manner not unlike that of William Miller, Russell and his followers announced their expectation that the Battle of Armageddon would be fought in a year certain—in Russell's calculations, 1914. And, as with the Adventists, the failure to see the anticipated events come to pass on the specified date resulted in defections from the movement. Strangely, a similar drama was repeated by the Witness faithful in 1925 and 1975. In all three cases, explanations have been offered about events that were alleged to have occurred in heaven on the dates in question. Those explanations were sufficient to retain members.

Jehovah's Witnesses have a preference for using Jehovah as the name for God. Jehovah is not a biblical name; it is a construct based on the Hebrew *YHWH* (pronounced by Christians as *Yahweh*), married to the vowels from *Adonai*,[25] to produce *Yahowah*, or in English—*Jehovah*.

Witnesses look to the Bible as their authority, but their teaching strays far from the biblical positions of orthodox Christianity. Russell exerted leadership over the Bible Study Movement for nearly forty years, founding several periodicals, notably *Zion's Watchtower* and *Herald of Christ's Presence*. He saw no need to create a structure beyond the Bible study movement to carry on his work—this despite the fact that his followers organized themselves after a fashion, meeting together to study the Bible and Russell's views as reported and explained in his publications.

On his death in 1916, the only title Charles Russell claimed was president of *Zion's Watchtower and Tract Society*, a post he had assumed in 1884. He was succeeded in 1917 by Judge Joseph Rutherford. If Russell's style was quiet and unassuming, Judge Rutherford's was virtually the opposite. Early in his leadership, Rutherford engaged in activities that created conflict with the Board of *Zion's Watchtower and Tract Society*. After dismissing four board members who he claimed were illegally elected, he released a publication which he falsely claimed had been written by Russell before his death. When the publication's true authorship was discovered, the Society splintered, but Judge Rutherford remained in control of the main body of the Bible Study Movement.

In 1918, citing his opposition to support of US participation in World War I, the US government brought an action against Rutherford and his new board of directors. They were found guilty of violating the Espionage Act and sentenced to serve twenty years in prison. The attitude of American citizens toward those who, during World War I, did not support military action against the Central Powers was virulent. In less than a year, however, Rutherford and his followers were released and their convictions reversed.

Rutherford was unflinching and unyielding in his effort to exert total control over the Bible Study Movement and *Zion's Watchtower and Tract Society*. In 1925, he relieved members of the Society's Editorial Committee of all duties. Earlier, he had appointed a director for each congregation and a year later (1920) required that all those who "preached"—that is, those who went door-to-door seeking to win converts—would report on their work to headquarters on a weekly basis.

In 1932, the Bible study movement adopted the name *Jehovah's Witnesses*. The next year saw the right to elect their own elders taken away from the local congregations. The leadership, located in Brooklyn, New York, came to grant Judge Rutherford near total control over the organization, the members, the publications, and the group's doctrines.

With "end-times" central to the doctrines of Jehovah's Witnesses, their message was skewed toward such topics as the kingdom of God, the role to be played by Jesus in the world to come, and the path to salvation for members. Among their positions:

- Jehovah and Jesus are quite separate from one another.

- Although Jehovah promised Jesus that he would rule over God's kingdom, Jesus was not enthroned as King until 1914 (see above) after a nearly 2000-year wait.

- Some "faithful men and women" from earth will go to heaven and will rule with Jesus as kings, judges, and priests; there are 144,000 such persons (cf. Revelation 14).

- When Jesus assumed the throne in God's kingdom, he cast Satan and his angels out of heaven, a cause of the earth's troubles since 1914.

- Jesus will, at some future date, judge people, separating them as a shepherd might "cull" out goats—i.e., those who have failed to accept God's message. They will be destroyed; the sheep will enjoy eternal life on earth.

- God's kingdom will replace all earthly kingdoms; people will live at peace.

- Jesus will reign for a thousand years; faithful people will become perfect. The earth will be a paradise. Jesus will hand the kingdom back to God.

- Death is a state of unconsciousness or nonexistence.

- Many members of Jehovah's Witnesses believe they will never die but will go directly to heaven or reign with Jesus on earth.

It is common for Jehovah's Witnesses to be made the subjects of extensive press coverage for their unwillingness to accept or allow blood transfusions. Parents who adhere to Witness beliefs about transfusions frequently have their refusal cited as a contributing factor to the death of their sick children. There are a handful of medical institutions and some doctors who accommodate the no transfusion rule in order to serve Witnesses.

Also, the subject of often critical press coverage is the position of Jehovah's Witnesses on military service. They have been painted as unpatriotic, even as ones who give aid and comfort to the enemy. In the most rigorous antiwar expression, Witness young people may even reject the option of serving as conscientious objectors.

In like fashion, members of Jehovah's Witnesses refuse to swear oaths, to stand for the singing of the national anthem, or to salute the flag. It is noteworthy that Jehovah's Witnesses in Germany were treated severely by the Nazis during World War II.

Leadership of Jehovah's Witnesses in the years subsequent to the death of Judge Rutherford has been, it is said, less confrontational. A major emphasis has been placed on training programs for members. The Witness-backed *New World Translation of the Holy Scriptures* was published in 1961; biblical scholars are critical of the translation.

Holidays that have a prominent place among orthodox Christian groups—Christmas, Easter, Halloween, Mother's Day—are not celebrated by Jehovah's Witnesses, nor are national holidays observed. They do observe annually a commemoration of Jesus's death on the date of Passover (Nisan 14). The commemoration is referred to as the Lord's Evening Meal.

Standards of personal behavior are strict: drunkenness, drug use, tobacco use, and gambling are proscribed. Divorce is forbidden, save for adultery; remarriage after a divorce for any other reason is considered adultery. The husband is the authority on all family matters. Homosexuality is forbidden; abortion is considered murder. All sex outside of marriage is grounds for disfellowshipping.

Jehovah's Witnesses report a membership of 7.1 million members worldwide in more than 103,000 congregations.[26] US membership is pegged at 1,114,009. Members can be excommunicated (their word is *disfellowshipped*) for serious sin, and witnesses are expected to shun those who have been disfellowshipped.

The demographic studies of religious groups undertaken by the Pew Forum show that Jehovah's Witnesses are to be found in all sections of the country with a southern and western "tilt." They are ethnically diverse—48 percent white, 22 percent black, 24 percent Hispanic. Both income and education of members are below national averages.

Seventh-day Adventists

At approximately the same time and in the same general geographic region as the one in which Joseph Smith experienced his revelations, a New York farmer and Baptist lay leader, William Miller, predicted the return of Jesus Christ to earth. Miller was specific: the second coming of Jesus would take place between March 21, 1843, and March 21, 1844. He arrived at the dates after extensive study of Scripture and based his prediction on the 2,300 days to which mention is made in Daniel 8:14. Miller held that the text really meant 2,300 years. When the end didn't come in the window predicted, one of Miller's followers, Samuel Snow, argued that the "tarrying time," referred to in the book of Habbakuk (2:3), added seven months and ten days to the original prediction. Thus, October 22, 1844, became the date for the expected return of Christ. When that date also failed to produce the greatly anticipated event, many of Miller's followers faded away. The failure was referred to as the Great Disappointment. Some followers remained steadfast due to the strength of their commitments to the movement.

Some of Miller's followers came to believe that while all of his painstaking calculations had been accurate, the interpretation of the Daniel text—that Christ's scheduled return to earth on the date referred to in the text—had been mistaken. A subsequent explanatory doctrine was promulgated that held that the date in question referred to Christ's entry into the most holy place in heaven.

For nearly nineteen years, the Millerite movement was largely unorganized—there existed publications, *The Advent Review* and *Sabbath Herald*; Sabbath observance was practiced; and a charismatic woman, Ellen White, grew to prominence among the followers. But it was not until 1863 that the church was officially established with headquarters in Battle Creek, Michigan.

Ellen White's gifts proved important to the Millerites. Her visions led people to consider her a prophet, and her writings (cf. *Desire of Ages*) helped Adventists formulate coherent theological positions. Although her writings are considered authoritative, they remain subject to the teachings of the Bible. Some contemporary Adventist clergy and theologians seem less convinced of White's importance to the movement or of her authority than were the clergy in previous generations.

There are a few Seventh-day Adventist doctrines that may be described as unique to the movement. On the other hand, the majority of SDA teachings are not unlike those of orthodox Protestant Christianity—especially those of evangelical persuasion.

In 1980, the General Conference of the Seventh-day Adventist Church adopted twenty-eight fundamental beliefs of the church, augmented some years later by a twenty-ninth belief. These are not a creed; they are, however, the distinctive positions of the church. The Bible is the only SDA "creed"—sola Scriptura!

A few of the positions that may be uniquely associated with Seventh-day Adventists are:

- Sabbath should be observed on the seventh day.

- Humans are a unity of mind, body, and spirit; they do not possess an immortal soul.

- Death is an unconscious sleep.

- The wicked will not suffer eternal torment but will be destroyed.

- Christians are being examined (or are to be judged) to determine who is worthy of salvation.

Seventh-day Adventists are Trinitarian—they affirm that Father, Son, and Holy Spirit "comprise" one God. (This position was adopted after an early flirtation with Arianism.) The book of Genesis is without errors. God created the earth and all its life forms in six, twenty-four-hour days, less than 10,000 years ago—this despite the fact that the universe may be ancient. Salvation is by the grace of God through faith in Jesus Christ; faith should lead to action—e.g., baptism and adherence to moral laws. In practical terms, many modern forms of entertainment (theater, television, film) are to be avoided. The doctrine of original sin is affirmed. Arminianism—i.e., that man has free will—is the dominant theological posture.

In general terms, Seventh-day Adventists are in agreement with both the political agenda and behavioral standards of the evangelicals: homosexual behavior is forbidden, women are subordinate to men and do not serve in the highest church offices, abortion is forbidden in all but the most extreme circumstances, divorce is allowed only in the case of adultery or physical violence. Simplicity in dress and speech is promoted. A simple, quiet, restrained, and modest lifestyle is held to be desirable and is actively promoted.

SDA worship takes place on Saturday. Sabbath school is available to children, youth, and adults. The service which follows is one with which most Protestants—especially those from non-liturgical churches—would find familiar: hymn singing, Scripture reading, prayers, and a sermon are standard. A freewill offering is received.

Four times a year, Adventists celebrate communion. Unlike most Christian churches, their service commences with the ordinance of foot washing, which is intended to illustrate the need for humility. Members may be segregated by sex for the foot washing. The Lord's Supper follows the foot washing; the elements are unleavened bread and grape juice.

Seventh-day Adventists have a long history of promoting healthy behavior. From the earliest years, they have recommended a vegetarian lifestyle, and while members are not required to be vegetarians, an extensive program of education promotes the value of the recommended diet: whole grain breads, cereals, vegetables and fruit, beans, nuts, etc. Among their claims: "Vegetarian men under forty can expect to live eight years longer and women more than seven years longer than the general population."[27] SDA members are discouraged from using alcohol, tobacco, or illegal drugs; some are known to avoid coffee, tea, and caffeine-containing soft drinks.

The Seventh-day Adventist Church is democratic in both style and practice. The local church is comprised of members, male and female, who have been baptized. They have voice and vote. Beyond the local church is the local conference (sometimes referred to as the local mission), which is comprised of local churches and their delegates within a given state or province. The local conference owns the church property, appoints ministers, and distributes contributions in such manner as to provide for clergy salaries and other expenses. The conference is, typically, a participant in a union conference which may comprise several states. The highest SDA organization is the General Conference located in Silver Springs, Maryland. The General Conference is the authority; it has the final say on all administrative and theological issues.

In the local church, lay leaders occupy the positions of elders and deacons. Selected by vote of the membership, elders have a responsibility to provide spiritual leadership to the membership in the absence of the minister and to maintain oversight of church activities. Deacons are to provide practical charitable services to member or friends and to oversee the physical properties of the congregation. It is notable that SDA polity at the local level and beyond is not unlike the polity operative in churches of the Reformed tradition.

The Seventh-day Adventist Church gives evidence of its commitment to education by operating schools, colleges, and universities serving a million and a half students located throughout the world. Their interest in health takes shape in the 54 U.S. hospitals and 167 the church operates worldwide. Since the end of the Second World War, Adventists have played a prominent role in activities that deliver aid to persons in need. The agency created by the church to provide relief in crisis situations in more than one hundred countries is the Adventist Development and Relief Agency, which has garnered the respect of and a special status with United Nations Education, Scientific, and Culture Organization (UNESCO).

The Seventh-day Adventist Church is open to and active among so-called minority populations and poor or developing nations in South America, Africa, and Asia.

The church has experienced a number of schisms in its nearly 150-year history. The most publicized such group in recent years is the Branch Davidian, which, under David Koresh, became a scandal culminating in the Waco, Texas, siege and led to the deaths of seventy-six of Koresh's adherents. Other defections have focused largely on interpretations of the atypical doctrines promulgated by the SDA church.

The large and growing impact of the Adventists is apparent in the fact that they are to be found in over two hundred countries in the world. Fewer than 10 percent of Seventh-day Adventist Church members are to be found in North America. Others may disagree, but there is compelling evidence that with an 11 percent annual growth rate, they are the fastest growing church/religious group in the world.

The three movements here designated modern-day Gnostics all have active missionary programs aiming to convert persons to their respective faith commitments. That they have been successful in winning over the dissatisfied and/or vulnerable from mainline churches is clear from both the raw numbers and from the demographics. While all three have their origins in the United States, all are now active and successful on an international scale.

Not all of the challenges to the churches of historic Protestantism set God at the center of their lives.

Atheists, Agnostics, and Secularists

Disagreement with the idea that a god exists who can and does engage with humans has existed for centuries—albeit as a minority view. Disbelief is not something new. It seems, however, to have become more prevalent and its adherents more public in recent years. And atheism has, without question, won converts in the last quarter century among some who have had roots in the mainstream Christian churches. One recent study has found that 1.6 percent of the population of the United States is atheist.[28]

In recent years three books have attained the status of bestsellers contending for the atheist gospel: Richard Dawkins's *The God Delusion*, Sam Harris's *Letter to a Christian Nation*, and Christopher Hitchens's *God Is Not Great*. Among the authors, one is a prominent, highly regarded evolutionary biologist; another, a full-time author; and the third, a brilliant journalistic controversialist. Although their published works differ from one another in significant ways, their arguments and the arguments of other contemporary atheists are sufficiently similar to permit a fair summary of the postmodern atheist position.

Plainly, these three cited are not the only persons contending for atheism in recent years. They stand with such men as Einstein, Hawkins, and Sagan, whose works were published some years ago and with others—Daniel Dennett, for example—whose works are more recent.

Among the similarities one finds in the works of the recent bestselling threesome, and many others of like mind, is their disdain of Christian fundamentalism and evangelicalism on both theological and political fronts. That disdain may indeed have served to motivate their public defense, if not their embrace, of atheism.

A definition is useful before proceeding: atheism stands over against theism, the belief in the Creator of the universe who continues to involve himself with the universe and all that is in it. The theist God is involved with humans in that he has expectations of human behavior—rewarding and punishing, forgiving sins, and answering prayers. Atheists deny all of that, although they may, on occasion, invoke the term *god*, which is usually meant in a deist, pantheist, or panentheist sense.

The Judaeo-Christian Bible is held in contempt by modern-day atheists, and they frequently identify it as one of the reasons for their unbelief. The bloodthirsty

God of the Old Testament, Yahweh, is cited for his bizarre expectations of man, for the killing he demands of his followers, for his capriciousness in changing his mind, his preoccupation with the nation of Israel. The Bible itself is cited for its contradictions (let's see, did Noah take two of every kind into the ark, or was it seven?), its strange stories (man from mud, woman from a rib), its miraculous emphases (stopping the sun in the sky, besting the prophets of Baal at the altar), the earth's creation in six days (it took a lot longer than that, and how come there are two distinct contradictory creation stories in Genesis?), and so on.

No effort is made by these atheists to take into account the literary/historical criticism of Scripture which marks modern biblical studies. The findings of those studies that show convincingly that many men representing varying interests contributed to the Old Testament are not mentioned, let alone credited by the authors. When so-called "liberal or moderate" Christians are referenced in their works, the liberals and moderates are sloughed off as unnecessary, mistaken, naïve.

> There is, we are assured, a vast and beautiful terrain between atheism and religious fundamentalism that generations of Christians have quietly explored. According to liberals and moderates, faith is about mystery, and meaning, and community, and love …. Here we need only observe that the issue is both simpler and more

urgent than liberals and moderates generally admit. Either the Bible is just an ordinary book written by mortals, either Christ was divine, or he was not. ... If the Bible is an ordinary book and Christ an ordinary man, the history of Christian theology is the story of bookish men passing a collective delusion.

Harris, *Letter to a Christian Nation*

The idea that the Bible is without error (or inerrant—choose your word) is anathema to today's atheists as it is to many—perhaps most—educated persons. The claim of inerrancy and/or infallibility is advanced by fundamentalists and evangelicals alike and by Mormons, Adventists, and Jehovah's Witnesses. They are apt to query others with "Do you believe in the Bible?" more frequently than with "Do you believe in God?" Infallibility is, sad to say, even put forward by some in the mainline churches where biblical education has been sorely lacking, neglected, or has been flat-out wrong.

Nowhere on the battlefield between faith and skepticism has the fight been waged more politically than over the biblical story of creation. Warriors on both sides of the creation/evolution argument take no prisoners. In the simplest terms, creationists take the stories in the early chapters of Genesis as received truth. Some in the creationist camp go so far as to insist that the universe, and all that is within it, was created only six thousand years ago—if there were dinosaurs on earth, they lived alongside man.

On the other side, those persuaded by the findings of science point to the evolutionary process by which simple organisms mutated into more complex organisms in the process of which useful traits which had arisen or been developed in one generation of beast are passed on to succeeding generations. They show the huge spans of time required of the evolutionary process and the archaeological evidence that the earth has existed for millions of years.

School boards and teachers have sought to promote the truths of evolution only to find themselves in bitter conflict with persons claiming to be Christian insisting that evolution is "only a theory" (misunderstanding, in the process, the use of the term *theory* in science). "The Bible is true," they say; "the creation story is reportorially accurate." Protests and pickets, court cases, and news articles have kept the creationist/evolutionist controversy in this nation's consciousness for decades. Despite the time and energy committed to the controversy, a recent Gallup poll cited by Sam Harris holds that "…only 12 percent of Americans believe that life on earth has evolved through a material process without the interference of a deity…and 53 percent of Americans are actually creationists."[29]

The argument has seen a relatively recent metamorphosis on the part of the creationist side as some have proffered the idea of intelligent design. According to their view, Darwinism may, in fact, prove to be a more or less accurate description of how the animal world came to develop, but behind and underneath it all, there was the Creator intelligently designing the universe. Most scientists are profoundly uncomfortable with the idea of intelligent design, maintaining that it is another myth aimed at preserving the idea of a Creator and that there are many things in the universe that are *not* all that intelligently designed.

It should be noted that not all who claim the name of Christ are to be found on the side of the biblical literalists when it comes to creation. Many of the members and leaders of the mainline churches have set themselves in the corner of the evolutionists and have done so while holding to the historic faith. The Episcopal Church in the United States in 2005 issued "A Catechism of Creation: An Episcopal Understanding" that was prepared by the Committee on Science, Technology, and Faith of the Executive Council and commended for study in congregations. In that work, the Episcopal Church comes down, firmly and creatively, on the side of the scientific explanation of the origins of the universe.

Many of today's atheists hold that only science and the evidence made available for science to explore can provide an answer to the question "Does God exist?" Their position is that God does not exist. There is no scientific evidence of his existence. Many of the articulate atheists persist in the view that only the application of scientific methodology can determine whether God does or does not exist. Lacking specific evidence for God's existence, atheists feel justified he/she doesn't exist.

In a 2008 column in the *New York Times*, columnist David Brooks summarized what he called "the militant materialism of some modern scientists."

> To these self-confident researchers, the idea that the spirit might exist apart from the body is just ridiculous. Instead, everything arises from atoms. Genes shape temperament. Brain chemicals shape behavior. Assemblies of neurons create consciousness. Free will is an illusion. Human beings are 'hard-wired' to do this or that. Religion is an accident.[30]

Among the tactics of the latter-day atheists, a frontal attack has been mounted on the classic philosophical/theological arguments for the existence of God. Dawkins devotes an entire chapter and many additional scattered pages in *The God Delusion* to debating these arguments. Thomas Aquinas's five "proofs" are dismissed as "vacuous."

Three of those proofs are, I submit, epistemological—resting, as they do, on the workings of human knowledge. These three constitute, in a word, the same argument set in three different ways: the unmoved movers, the uncaused cause, the cosmological argument. They go like this: Nothing moves without a mover. Unless one posits God as the mover, we are faced with an infinite regress, and that is, quite simply, unthinkable. Nearly 2,500 years ago, Plato took this position. Dawkins, and others of like mind, argue that if infinite regress is unthinkable, God himself must be seen as subject to the same fate. Where did he come from?

The argument for God's existence to which philosophers and theologians give the name *the ontological argument* was first voiced by Anselm, the twelfth-century archbishop of Canterbury. It is an argument that modern-day atheists dismiss—even deride. Anselm reasoned that there must be an argument for God's existence that does not rely, for confirmation or proof, on Scripture or authority. He prayed for such an argument, and the answer came in a flash: God is something than which nothing greater can be conceived. A being that doesn't exist is less than perfect. Ergo, God exists.

The argument is, or seems to be, verbal trickery and thus an absurdity when dealing as it does with so important an issue as the existence of deity. Nonetheless, Anselm's syllogism tends to be dusted off and restated again and again in each generation. Even Dawkins quotes Bertrand Russell, who he declares is no fool: "It is easier to feel convinced that the ontological argument must be fallacious than it is to find out precisely where the fallacy lies."[31]

Today's atheists are fond of citing the vast majority of scientists who do not believe in God's existence. There is no gainsaying their ability with numbers, the overwhelming preponderance of scientists who are atheists or agnostics. What else is to be expected of men and women who have been taught and who have given over their lives to the idea that material evidence must exist for anything that may be said to be real:

rules or laws, stars or atoms, elements or electrons, or God? They stand in line with such men as W. K. Clifford, who wrote, in 1879, "… it is monstrous, immoral, and perhaps even impolite to accept a belief for which you have insufficient evidence."[32] And Lord Kelvin is reported to have said, "When you can measure what you are speaking about and express it in numbers, you know something about it."[33]

Christians, especially fundamentalist and evangelical Christians, cite with equal vigor the scientists who are, or who seem to be, people of faith. They claim, and celebrate, such Christian scientists as Francis Collins, who leads the Human Genome Project, and John Polkinghorne, physicist and Anglican priest. They even try, on occasion, to claim that Albert Einstein was a man of faith, although he famously said, "I am a deeply religious nonbeliever," and on many other occasions denied belief in a personal deity.

When all is said about today's atheists—arguments against the classic "proofs" of God's existence, materialist tendencies, and the search for evidence—the factors that cause their temperatures to rise are Christian fundamentalist and evangelical beliefs and actions and the political agenda to which they are committed.

If Atheists are noteworthy for the strength of their convictions and the *certainty* of their unbelief, agnostics are noteworthy for their tentativeness. The word *agnostic* is based on the Greek *gnosis*, which translates as *knowledge*; with the "a" prefixed, it means no knowledge or lack of knowledge. Thomas Henry Huxley, one of Darwin's collaborators, is credited with coining the word in the 1860s. A recent study concluded that about 2.4 percent of the United States population is agnostic—about 50 percent more agnostics as atheists.[34]

There are a variety of circumstances to which agnosticism may be claimed. These three are significant for our purposes:

> Of greater moment. "I do not know if there is life after death."
>
> The manner in which the term is typically used. "I do not know whether God exists—there is no verifiable evidence, but I am prepared to grant there *may* be a deity."
>
> The adamant or atheistic agnostic. "There is no evidence for God, and I do not believe there can be a God."

Across the centuries, there have been many who have refused to commit to either belief or unbelief when deity is the subject. Bertrand Russell is perhaps the best known of the prominent "thinkers" of the twentieth century to have set forth the classic agnostic position:

> As a philosopher, if I were to speak to a purely philosophic audience I should say that I ought to describe myself as an Agnostic, because I do not think there is a conclusive argument by which one can prove that there is not a God.[35]

One suspects that not a few of the Founding Fathers of the United States—notably Jefferson and Madison—were agnostics and that their apparent interest in or dalliance with deism was a way of saying, "I simply don't know," to theistic claims.

On the broader philosophical front, Immanuel Kant and William Hamilton join Bertrand Russell in the agnostic camp, albeit in differing ways. Kant held that while absolute reality may exist, it is simply not knowable. And Hamilton insisted that all knowledge is relative and to know the Absolute is, therefore, impossible.

There is a kind of brutal honesty about the agnostic—"I simply don't (or can't) know; therefore, I can't commit"—that one doesn't often see in today's secularist. Their faith, if that's the right word, is placed in their own daily schedule. On the momentous questions about deity or immortality, the secularist doesn't seem to care. The Pew survey concludes that 12.1 percent of the population may be seen as secularists: 6.3 percent are identified as secular unaffiliated and 5.8 percent as religious unaffiliated.

The secularist believes or acts as though he/she believes that all he/she needs is right here in that which surrounds him/her: his/her things, job, bank account, politics, vacation, prospects for retirement. Admittedly, that is harsh. It should not be taken to mean that the secularist is evil or immoral. He/she may well have friends. He/she is not, by definition, a liar or a cheat. He/she can be a good parent, a loving mate. But it is likely that the secularist lives life on or near its surface, lacking a full-blown commitment to either the mind or the spirit, one in which intellect, mystery, community fail to work their way into a major role in the secularist's life drama.

The secularist is one who appears to make judgments about everything in which he/she comes in contact in terms of its effect on the self. By the very nature of secularism, the secularist is self-limiting. He/she may, if pushed, fall back on the canard "I am spiritual, not religious," thus relieving the self of anything more serious on Sunday or Christmas or Easter than a walk in the woods, a trip to the beach, a chocolate Santa, or a colored egg.

As atheism and agnosticism impact the mainline church and its adherents, the Pew Forum Poll reported that in the period 1990 to 2009 self-identified atheists and agnostics have grown in number from 1 million to 3.6 million—a function, no doubt, of the volume of books and articles supporting the atheist position.

The American Religious Identification Survey has reported that all forty-eight contiguous states were "less religious," as self-identified in 2008, than they were in 1990. The survey found that in the eighteen-year period, Christian churches added 22 million members to a total of more than 173 million, even as their portion of the nation's population shrank by 10 percent (86 percent to 76 percent).

Arguments about the existence of God and of his/her nature, if existent, have gone on for centuries. These arguments address huge issues impacting life at almost every point. Modern atheists and agnostics appear, in recent years, to have adopted a platform seeking to win persons to their point of view. They reason that the Christian faithful, or at least a significant portion of them, stand in the way of scientific truth. Their challenge to the churches is beginning to show some success.

Why Did They Go?

The data are compelling: For over four decades, the membership of the churches of the seven mainline denominations has been declining. To be sure, there is some "give and take" in the numbers of people on church rolls—people moving, members dying, families breaking up—and honesty requires that we admit that church membership statistics are notoriously inaccurate. But the unvarnished fact is that the mainline churches have not come close to replacing with new members those who have left. The most conservative estimates are that the mainline churches have lost one-fifth to one-third of their members in the last forty years, and some have lost many more.

In the chapter "Back in the Day," it was noted that some mainline church members were dismayed, angry with the activist role played by their clergy during the civil rights struggle, the war on poverty, and the anti-Vietnam War movement. With a strong sense that they had been victims of "bait and switch," members drifted away—or stormed away. "When we joined

First Church in 1948, it was for our family. Now the preachers are bringing politics into the pulpit. We don't support that." That was over forty years ago and does not—cannot—begin to explain the severe membership attrition the mainline churches have suffered in the ensuing years.

There are, it would appear, many reasons for the decline. Fortunately, the reasons have been researched by a number of good scholars; interestingly, more of the research seems to have been done by sociologists than by clergy scholars. One cleric who entered the discussion was the late Dean M. Kelley, who, in 1972, published *Why Conservative Churches Are Growing*. Controversial when it was published, that work by this longtime official of the National Council of Churches held that mainline churches were in decline because they had become weak. They tolerate, or even promote, a diversity of opinions on theological matters. Few members can state the basic doctrines of their church.[36] They do not promote a common discipline for their members. They have no rules of conduct—at least no enforced rules. The consequence is that membership in a mainline church has become little more than a hobby—maybe less—and means little in the grand scheme of the lives of many mainline church members.

In contrast, the fundamentalist and evangelical churches and others who are positioned off the mainstream are very sure and very clear about their faith distinctives and their commitment to those distinctives. Members are taught from the pulpit and in classes what their church believes, and it is made abundantly clear that those beliefs are to be seen as *revealed truth* and are not to be challenged.

In recent years, many mainline churches have embraced survival goals: growth for growth's sake. This is a tactic that says, by one means or another, get members in sufficient numbers and acquire income large enough to keep the doors open and the lights on. It is truly remarkable how infrequently the important questions are asked or answered, "Why should someone become an active member of this church? What will a member discover here about God? What does a member's relationship to God imply about his or her responsibilities?"

Other institutions—colleges, unions, businesses, hospitals, libraries, even clubs and voluntary associations—have learned that dependence on survival goals alone is self-limiting and ultimately self-defeating. Constituents will provide real strength to an institution to the degree that they know what the institution stands for and why they commit to it.

The Johnson, Hoge, and Ludens' 1995 study,[37] updated in 2002, was based on interviews with baby boomers who had been confirmed in the Presbyterian Church (USA) in the 1960s. Among their findings, this was, perhaps, the most stunning: "We found that fully 75 percent of our baby boom confirmands had dropped out of the church at one time or other, typically around age twenty-one, and that about half of the drop-outs are now active again in some church." It is noted that their definition of "active" is minimal: a boomer member who "attends church at least six times a year and is enrolled as a member."

Their study found that 52 percent of the baby boomer confirmands are currently churched. The status of the study subjects as of the date of the study:

Self-identified fundamentalists
6 percent

Members of other mainline church
10 percent

Members of other non-mainline churches
7 percent

Agnostics or atheists
8 percent

Currently active Presbyterians
29 percent

Members who do not attend
19 percent

"Religious" but neither belong nor attend
21 percent

Among the interesting and counterintuitive findings of the Johnson, Hoge, Ludens' study was that political issues played only a small part in motivating members to leave their mainline churches and a college education did not play a major part in motivating defection. Abortion and ordination of homosexual clergy are subjects of strong opinions but do not appear to be the cause of most of the movement away from the mainline church. What emerged as the "single best predictor of church participation" was orthodox Christian belief—*salvation through Christ alone*. Most of the boomers who accept that proposition are active members of one church or another; many who do not are not.

The schedule many Americans keep, or try to keep, has been put forward by some as a reason, perhaps *the* reason, that middle-class Americans have given up on their mainline church membership. Today's middle class family has work obligations that, we are told, have expanded rather than diminished in recent years in terms of the hours required to "do the job." And if there are children to raise, friends and family to see, hobbies or avocations to pursue, then church involvement will inevitably, for some, take a backseat.

Perhaps the Hadaway and Mailer study[38] (Chaves assisting) speaks to the business argument. They found that the 40 percent figure, long held to be standard for Protestant church attendance, was vastly overstated. For Protestant church members, the operative number was 20 percent (and for Catholics was only 25 percent). It would seem that for many church members, the game on television or the backyard barbeque has earned the "significantly more important" spot in the busy church member's life. Ultimately, that member may well decide that church membership is of little consequence in his/her hierarchy of values. It would seem that church attendance, like playing the violin, must be practiced if one is to get good at it.

Failure to find a sense of community in one's local congregation is without question the reason a large number of members seek a new place of worship. Similarly, failure to be comfortable with the existing sense of community in the subject congregation will provide some with a compelling reason to move on to another church or to leave the church altogether.

The reasons either of these types of breakdown of community may occur include: new pastoral or lay leadership; one or more members with whom one is in conflict; an influx of members who are unlike others in the congregation by reason of race, ethnicity, or political persuasion; changing social, economic, achievement status or academic attainment. Clearly, a sense of community ruptured by any of these factors is or could be troubling. Such ruptures can and do occur, and people do leave churches or change church membership based on such factors.

Yet another reason members have left their mainline congregation has to do with urbanization, the changing city, and suburbia. The years since World War II have witnessed the growing urbanization of America and the development of residential communities "farther out." As cities have grown, their populations have changed, and churches have had to adapt to new populations. As noted earlier, some mainline urban congregations have been remarkably successful in tailoring their ministries to their new neighbors. Most have not.

In one Southern California city of some 300,000 souls, there were thirteen Protestant churches in the center of the city forty years ago, most of them churches of mainline denominations. Today, only three of those churches remain, and at least one of them appears to be on life support. A relatively new and apparently thriving Pentecostal church has taken up quarters in a former real estate office in the neighborhood. A majority of the churches in that city moved to the suburbs, and their members have similarly sought out new residences in the suburbs. Frequently, the suburban choice of the church has not been the suburban choice of the transplanted members. *Presto*! There we have an apparently valid reason to change one's church membership.

A related factor is that in a society changing rapidly on many fronts, institutional loyalties tend to fray and grow weak. The churches of the mainline are, by the very fact of their histories, institutions affiliated with denominational entities. Their names betray those affiliations: First *Methodist* Church, St. Andrews *Presbyterian* Church, Messiah *Lutheran* Church, etc. To those affiliations, those institutions, growing numbers are saying, "I don't care what denomination a church is; I want it to speak to my needs, my interests." The result is clearly to be seen in the designations used by the churches of the Christian right: independent, non-denominational, community, etc. They are saying, by the use of such designations, "You need not be loyal to anything save the gospel and *this* church.

Failure to attract or hold young people provides many young families the reason to seek a different church. This reason takes many forms: There is the young single mother who loves the church of which she has been a member for many years but who feels compelled to join a different church—an evangelical church—because it has attracted more families with kids and she wants her own children to belong to a church in which other kids are involved. There is the family which maintains its membership in their mainline church but permits the teenage son to drop out of the family's church and join one that is crawling with kids. There is the girl who was an active church member until she went away to college but somehow, and for some unexplained or poorly understood reason, never returns to the church of her childhood and youth when her college days are behind her.

One of the reasons, of course, for the youth drain is that the membership of mainline churches skews older. The data gathered by the Pew Forum on Religion & Public Life indicates that nearly a quarter of the members of mainline churches are over the age of sixty-five, while less than a fifth of the members of evangelical churches are sixty-five or older. Of greater impact, however, may be the fact that evangelical churches seem to put front and center those activities which are thought to have appeal specific to significant numbers of teenage kids. It may be their music, their range of social/recreational activities, or their freer style of worship. The study, discipline, and straightforward message of the contemporary evangelical church appears to present the Christian gospel in a manner to which more young people respond than they do to a mainline church. How can the Methodist pastor compete for loyalty of the family of the nine-year-old girl from his Sunday school who is now attending an evangelical church nearby because they "have a rock wall to climb"?

Earlier in this chapter, we introduced Dean Kelley's conclusion that the mainline churches have lost members and momentum because they are weak. My observation is that a major factor favoring the churches contending for membership with the mainline is the lack of clear-cut authority. Kelley talks about discipline and the fact that theology or faith systems are subject to lay opinions so that there are no rules. At root, Kelley's argument is that in the apparent absence of real authority, the mainline churches have become flabby.

The evangelicals and fundamentalists know by what authority they preach and lead—the Bible. Their authority message is straightforward and direct: the Bible is without error; the Bible contains all that is needed for salvation. If one accepts Christ as Lord and Savior, he or she will be saved—i.e., will, after death, be spared an eternity in hell and will live forever in heaven with Jesus. There is no opportunity for confusion in that proclamation—that message is held to be right there in the pages of the Bible for all to see, and there is no arguing with the Bible. That is authority writ large!

When compared to that simple message, the mainline churches' take on authority and, therefore, on its message appears complicated and confusing:

- The Bible is *one* of the authoritative sources for the mainline churches, *but* one must take into account when it was written, by whom and to whom. Some of the Bible must be seen as myth. It often contradicts itself. There is some of it that is just god-awful bloodthirsty.

- Tradition is *another* source of authority in the mainline church. What did Augustine or Iraenaeus say? What can we learn from Luther and Calvin? Where do we find our faith in the words of more recent theologians—Niebuhr and Tillich, Borg and Crossan?

- The believer's own reason is a *third* authority for today's mainline member. "Utilizing my own intelligence *and* the Bible *and* tradition, what do I think of life after death, about Jesus—teacher, prophet—and how should I conduct myself as a mainline Christian?"

The undeniable conclusion is that it takes hard work to be a thoughtful, convinced, and convincing Christian of mainline church persuasion. It can be done and is being done by many, but that mark of Christian discipleship is ignored by many others. If the mainline church member is not prepared to struggle with the authority question, he/she may leave or, indeed, almost certainly will leave.

Compare the message about authority in the mainline (three different sources of authority) to the Catholics (the pope is infallible), to the Mormons ("the Twelve Apostles in Salt Lake will tell you what to believe"), to the Jehovah's Witnesses ("Your message will come directly from Brooklyn headquarters"), to the evangelicals (the Bible is infallible), to fundamentalists (the Bible is inerrant), to the atheists (evidence from the material world is the only thing that matters). It is small wonder that, when faced with a choice, some are bound to choose the simple and clear authority message of mainline's competitors over the "do it yourself!" authority which is required of members in the historic Protestant denominations.

The Johnson, et al., study gets at this very issue in a different way. They refer to what they call *lay liberalism,* a pattern of thought widespread in the mainline churches which rejects the idea that Christianity is the only true religion. Its practitioners/adherents do not subscribe to any particular theological school of thought. Rather, they tend to believe that all religions proclaim basically the same message, that the Bible and the Quran were equally inspired by God. Lay liberals are of the opinion that all religions teach a common morality and that God dooms no one to hell. They are nervous about efforts of their mainline church to seek to convert any one to the Christian faith. "What's the point? All religions are the same." In short, theirs is a religion largely without content and unlikely to endure for another century, let alone another two thousand years.

The observations about the amorphous faith of the lay liberals are supportive of the argument that mainline church members don't recognize the authority of their church, don't even subscribe to the idea that there is authority in the message of the mainline church. When everyone's opinions are valued and defended, however vapid they may be and however antithetical to historic Christian thought they are, then the gospel message ceases to have meaning. The exercise of authority by each Christian (Bible, tradition, reason) is the foundation on which strength and power is created in the mainline churches and on which a future can be built, but when was the last time your mainline preacher stressed that fact?

> The basic affirmation of the New Testament is that God took human form in Jesus Christ ... Paul's Letter to the Philippians declares that the eternal Christ, not taking equality with God for granted, "revealed God in human shape" (Phil 4:8, NEB) ... Here is the suggestion that God is not ultimately concerned with religion or religious people. He is not ultimately concerned with ministers or buildings or Church programs

or congregations. He shaped himself into human
life so that true humanity could emerge.[39]

It would appear that this gospel message is not believed
or known or heard or even recognized by all too many
members of mainline churches. Are the clergy not proclaiming from the pulpit the message that "God was in
Christ" reconciling the world to himself? Are there no
adult classes teaching the doctrine and meaning of the
incarnation? Are parents not exposed to the authentic
content of Christian doctrine when they present their
children for baptism? Are candidates denied knowledge of God's action prior to confirmation? Must we
look to the evangelical churches for a clear, uncompro-
mising proclamation of the gospel?

A recent analysis of the teaching of the humanities
in American universities is analogous to the preaching
of the gospel in the mainline churches. William M.
Chace, past president of Wesleyan and Emory Universities, notes that humanities majors have declined
precipitously in the last thirty years—in cases by more
than 50 percent. Addressing, specifically, the decline in
English majors, Chace writes,

> What are the causes of this decline? There
> are several, but at the root is the failure of
> departments of English across the country to
> champion, with passion, the books they teach
> and to make a strong case to undergraduates that
> the knowledge of those books and the tradition

in which they exist is a human good ... What departments have done is ... substitute for the books themselves a scattered array of secondary considerations (identity studies, obtuse theory, sexuality, film and popular culture).[40]

To the degree that Presbyterians and Methodists and other of the historic Protestant denominations fail to proclaim the core Christian message (God was in Christ), they will continue to see their members drift away to other ecclesiastical manifestations of the Christian gospel. Is it too much to expect the mainline churches to proclaim the authentic gospel message?

Dean Kelley's conclusion that the mainline churches have lost traction with their members because they are weak is, or ought to be, a frightening indictment. The members have a right to know why they belong to a given church, and they should be able to articulate the reason(s). If they don't know and/or can't talk about their faith in a cogent manner, the leadership—the clergy—needs to seek God's forgiveness. Without question, the mainline churches must embark on a comprehensive strategy of education of those who are their members and those who may become their members.

The More We Get Together...

Author of *The Purpose Driven Life*, pray-er at the inauguration of President Obama, minister of Saddleback Church, and champion of the Christian right, Rick Warren, in 2009, expressed the wish that the mainline churches might come over and join evangelical churches in ministry and mission. Warren is not alone in his vision of a merged (mainline and evangelical) church. His wish/invitation rested on recognition that the mainline denominations are in decline so far as membership and influence are concerned and his confidence in and commitment to the strength of modern evangelicalism.

The impulse for Christians of varying points of view to make common cause with Christians of other points of view has a long and complex history. The high priestly prayer of Jesus, reported in John 17, was almost surely remembered and recorded by the gospel writer in response to tensions in the primitive church. Not only had Peter and James been at odds with Paul and Barnabas, but controversy among the faithful in the early years of the church was virtually endemic: Gnostics and magicians competed with apostolic Christians about the nature and work of Christ. "That all may be one" (John 17:20) was not only a fervent hope; it was a strategy for winning followers to an understanding that was consistent with the apostolic tradition.

Any reflection on the history of the church in the first millennium will come across those who claimed Christ but who tilted in a slightly (or significantly) different direction from others of the faith: Marcion and Hermas, Augustine and Mani, Methodius and the Donatists. Sometimes these differences resulted in name-calling, heresy charges, shunning, and even death. Always there was the conviction that if only all Christians would come together, it would be good for the cause of Christ.

Think of the conflict over the filioque clause in the Nicene Creed between Rome and Constantinople that led to the Great Schism in 1054. There were years of two popes—and then three. In the sixteenth century, the Reformation challenged not only the church but sundered the paradigm of church and state that had shaped Western civilization for more than a thousand years.

Since the Reformation, Christians have gone this way and that, all striving in their own ways to be faithful to the gospel but insisting on the truth of their own message: Catholics and Quakers, Mennonites and Lutherans, Calvinists and Free Methodists,

Episcopalians and Baptists. Some Roman Catholic historians have insisted that no heresy has ever lasted for more than four hundred years, yet here Protestant Christians are (heretics?) approaching a half a millennium of life, with statistical studies revealing that some groups among us are growing even as others seem to be shrinking.

Through these two thousand years, effort upon effort has been mounted to bring together groups claiming to be Christian but holding points of view that differed from others about the nature of the church, decision making in the church, the person and work of Christ, the relationship of Father to Son and to the Holy Spirit, the authority of Scripture, the nature of heaven and hell, the parousia, the Eucharist, etc. It would be wrong to suggest that all of the efforts of Christians to find and/or make common cause have failed: Roman Catholic efforts to deal with differences by recognizing differing monastic orders and limiting their roles (and carefully watching over them from Rome) have had a measure of success in limiting discord. And the historic councils of the church have served to bring order to both beliefs and practices.

In the churches of historic Protestantism (joining with the Anglican and Orthodox communities) such manifestations of the desire for unity as the International Conference on Life and Work, and the International Conference on Faith and Order, both held in 1937, worked for unity on issues related to social justice, missionary activities, ethics, theology, and ministry. Those conferences laid the foundation for the organization that was to become the World Council of Churches in 1948.

The Federal Council of Churches of Christ in the United States, formed in 1907; its inheritor, the National Council of Churches succeeding in 1950[41]; the scores of local Councils of Churches spread across this land and (sometimes by other names) across North and South America, Africa, Europe, and Asia—all have committed energy, financial resources, and good-will to healing the wounds of division.

Most of those efforts for Christian unity have had a federated quality about them. It is as though leaders have said, "Recognizing and holding on to our differences, let us find ways to share some of our ministries." The result has been cooperation without overturning distinctives. There have been some important mergers across denominational and confessional lines: The United Church of Christ (bringing together Congregationalists and Evangelical and Reformed churches with widely different histories and polities); the church of South India (involving Presbyterian, Congregational, and Episcopal polities and churches); the United Church of Canada (excluding Anglicans and Baptists but involving Methodists, Congregationalists, and about two-thirds of the Presbyterians).

The emerging strength of the Christian gospel in Africa and of varying branches of Protestantism in Central and South America holds promise for efforts in those regions to bring together separated churches in the coming decades.

The ecumenical thrust has been driven, in large measure, by a longing to be one with other Christians. Where formal mergers have been brought to pass, they have been preceded by negotiations which resulted in theological agreements, sometimes referred to as a "basis of union." While the specific content of the theological consensus has differed from case to case, it almost always addressed: the attitude of the involved parties toward the Bible, the person, and work of Christ as articulated in the historic creeds, the two sacraments ordained by Christ himself, and church polity. In those circumstances in which neither union nor federation have been achieved, it has often been because of disagreements on the subject of polity—i.e., will the leadership stand in the apostolic succession?

Given the history and conviction of the mainline churches in the United States and of the fundamentalist and evangelical churches, any effort of the one to incorporate or merge with the other seems fraught with difficulty and, on the surface, doomed to failure.

1. Their respective views of Scripture differ in important ways. The fundamentalist churches and their leaders hold rigidly to the view that the Judaeo-Christian Scriptures are inerrant, accurate in a reportorial sense. Little attention is paid, and no allowance is made for apparent impossibilities growing

out of pre-scientific myth-making ("the sun stood still," Joshua 10:13) or contradictions (two animals of every kind into the ark or seven?). Fundamentalists, as a general rule, are highly critical of evangelicals for their "lower view" of Scripture.

Evangelical clergy and churches characteristically display a reluctance to embrace the historical/critical approach to the study of Scripture and are prone to distance themselves from any language that implies acceptance of higher criticism as a way of dealing with Scripture. As a consequence, they refrain from uttering the word *inerrant* and argue instead that the Bible was inspired by God and is "infallible" in laying out God's path to salvation.

Clergy of the mainline churches who have studied in the seminaries of the mainline were introduced to the Graf-Wellhausen approach to the Old Testament and its argument for multiple authorships of the books of the Hexateuch. They are agreed that some of the other books of the Old Testament (e.g., Job, Isaiah) had more than one author and were written at different times marked by widely differing political circumstances.

On the subject of New Testament studies, mainline clergy, in the main, have bought into the "Q" analysis of the Synoptic Gospels and may favor later dating than their evangelical brethren of some of the books of the New Testament. While not all mainline clergy count themselves comfortable with Rudolf Bultman's "demy-thologizing" of the New Testament, they are likely to have been exposed to it during their seminary days. And they will have learned something of *formengeschichte* (form criticism) and have perhaps introduced that approach in the adult education classes and/or sermons that mark their ministries.

The predilection of fundamentalists and many evangelicals to see the book of Revelation as a (or *the*) predictor of future world events, especially as those events might relate to the earthly return of Jesus (premillennial?, postmillennial?, Rapture?, etc.), has virtually no place in the theology of mainline clergy.

While the varying attitudes toward the Bible are, for the short term, at least, a deal killer when it comes to a mainline/evangelical merger, they will not, in and of themselves, forestall some form of cooperation.

2. On the question of the person and work of Christ, fundamentalists, evangelicals, and mainline churchmen might very well be closer than they are on the subject of Scripture. After all, they share the historic creeds of the church and the catechisms and confessions written over the years, all of which offer answers to questions of faith in Christ as Lord and Savior.[42]

There are, of course, profound differences in how such a phrase is interpreted across the Christian spectrum.

Does it imply support of the doctrine of substitutionary atonement? What does such a statement say, or imply, about the doctrine of the Trinity? How is the Holy Spirit accounted for in the "Lord and Savior" (or "God and Savior") phrase?

And, of course, right in the midst of the subject of the person and work of Christ is the issue of the virgin birth and the complex of issues related to Mary, the mother of Jesus. The belief structure of fundamentalists, evangelicals, Pentecostalists, Jehovah's Witnesses, and Seventh-day Adventists alike make a critical issue of belief in the virgin birth of Jesus. Some might say, *the* critical issue. If Jesus was not born of a virgin, to which the gospels of both Matthew and Luke seem to testify, then what can we believe about the Jesus presented in the gospels?

While many mainstream clergy gladly and forthrightly attest to belief in the virgin birth—perhaps a sizeable majority—fewer would make of the virgin birth the critical issue touching on the person of Jesus. They would be more likely to argue that the work of Jesus Christ is more important than the manner in which he came into this world. Frustrated and impatient evangelicals (and others) are tempted to say, "If we can't believe what the Bible says about Jesus's birth, then everything else it says about him is open to question."

The place of Jesus Christ in the punishment-for-sin scenario—so important to the message of the mainline church's competitors—is one that is wholly discomfiting to many mainline clergy. The God of redeeming love is hard to reconcile with the eternal hell proclaimed by much of the Christian right. It is true that today, many in the fundamentalist/evangelical camp refrain from figuratively casting sinners into Satan's fires, arguing instead that separation from the love of God is the inevitable and awful fate awaiting sinners.[43] Still, the punishment dimension of the argument, coupled with the eternity frame, finds scant support among the mainline clergy.

In his review of David Hempton's recent book, *Evangelical Disenchantment: Nine Portraits of Faith and Doubt*, Todd Shy writes,

The most damning critique of evangelicalism in the book is the charge that its portrait of God is morally problematic, that evangelicals portray God as dictatorial, arbitrary, harsh .... God seemed to do things that were cruel and unusual.[44]

3. The overall political agenda of the Christian right has relatively little support among the churchmen of the mainstream. Opposition to abortion, to same sex marriage, to stem cell research and therapy, to no place in the church's ministry for sexually active gay clergy, for support of a subordinate role for women in the home and community all have been made out by fundamentalists and evangelicals to be standards on which a person can be judged Christian or not.

It is doubtlessly true that many in the mainstream churches find themselves in support of one or more of the positions in the right's political agenda; far fewer would endorse all of them. These positions, or many of them, have come to be identified with the Republican Party, a fact that has proven troublesome for church and party alike. The statistics tell the story: more active church members self-identify as Republicans; the mainline churches are comprised of lots of Republicans, at least some of whom disagree with the positions outlined above, the consequent disconnect between what I believe and how I vote harms the Republican Party, even as it makes for confusion and concern about church and society issues.

There are many moral/ethical questions facing the nation and its churches today that are in danger of being ignored by faith-based institutions and persons because the content of the fundamentalist/evangelical political agenda has given new life to the old (and manifestly incorrect) charge that because of separation of church and state, churches may not make political judgments or actively pursue ends perceived to be righteous by political means. Were such a position to have been enforced in past decades, there would have been no civil rights revolution followed by supportive legislation, no war on poverty, no end to the Vietnam War.

Some of the social issues on which evangelicals and the mainline ought to find agreement sufficient to justify collaboration are a comprehensive policy on immigration; the expansion of health care for the young, the poor, the elderly; responsible use of the planet and its resources; an end to human trafficking; and a foreign policy vision that does not lightly resort to the use of arms.

Evangelicalism is powered by high energy, and there remains significant energy in the mainline churches. Cooperation and collaboration on such issues as these could be the arena in which Christians may come together, and it could be the most important one.

4. The nature and practice of ordained ministry is yet another issue in which the differences between and among the mainline churches and the fundamentalist, evangelical, Pentecostal, and Gnostic churches are so deep as to present a serious challenge to collaboration and/or merger. The apostolic succession is one dimension of this challenge. It is not the only one.

The path to ordination set forth by the mainline churches, viz. university and seminary education, has been identified in other places. Many of the mainline's competitors recommend a similar (or even the same) pattern of study in preparation for ordination. The conflict comes in the answer to the question "Who ordains?" In the mainline churches, the ordaining entity almost always is a denominational judicatory; in the fundamentalist and evangelical churches, the ordaining entity is often the local church—and sometimes just a part of a local church.

A judicatory may differ as to authority and power in the mainline. For Presbyterians it is the Presbytery, and they tend to possess both power and authority. Ditto for Methodists and the District. For the United Church of Christ, the American Baptists, and the Disciples of Christ, the ordaining entity is the association in cooperation with the local church which tends to embody all of the traditions for fellowship and mutual support; ordination and the steps leading to it are often the only real power the association can exercise. For the Evangelical Lutherans, ordination policy is based on a national standard promulgated by the Division for Ministry. Those standards are implemented by a Synodical Candidacy Committee to screen applicants. Following approval, candidates are "approved for call." Bishops suggest names of potential pastors to congregations with pastoral vacancies. Candidates may not be ordained until they have received their first call. Ordination in the Episcopal Church is the responsibility of the diocesan bishop, usually with the advice of the Commission on Ministry of the diocese. In every case among the mainline churches, ordination is a function of a formal structure within the denomination.

When it comes to "nondenominational" churches, "Bible" churches, or "independent" churches, the rites associated with ordination may be, and often are, undertaken by a local pastor who may or may not choose to consult with lay leaders or fellow clergy.

Ordination has sometimes been granted by Bible study groups. American religious history contains painful examples of boys as young as ten or twelve years of age being ordained to ministry by one or more local church ministers.

Ordination in a mainline church should be seen as a step in a process that involves guidance, counseling, and testing. It usually requires several years—three years would be a minimal amount of time and often stretches to five, six, or seven years. Certainly ordination by a nondenominational fundamentalist or evangelical church is likely to have included some form of guidance and counsel and maybe an ordination paper and/or sermon and prayer. And on occasion, other like-minded churches will have been invited to share in the "laying on of hands." Even under those circumstances, ordination will have been an act of a local church.[45]

The ordaining entity is important for discipline. When a clergyman or woman engages in behavior that is inconsistent with his/her calling, or is illegal, immoral, unethical, or exploitative, that minister is, or should be, subject to discipline up to, and including, defrocking the subject minister. If an intermediate step is chosen, he/she may be required to take a leave from the practice of ministry, subject to appropriate conditions (e.g., psychotherapy) and oversight. The point is, whatever discipline is decided upon, in the mainline churches an entity exists whose responsibility it is to impose discipline.

When the entity is a local church, the disciplining role is difficult in the extreme! The offending party may have moved to another state to practice his/her ministry. The ordaining local church may never know of the moral, ethical, or legal failings that should require discipline and, thus, be unable to invoke it.

The principle here is that ordained ministry is a function of the Church, capital *C*, and should involve a process that draws as much of the church as practicable into the acts associated with ordination.

The nature and practice of ministry while presenting serious challenges are not issues that out-of-hand preclude deep cooperation and even merger of some of the mainline churches with some evangelical churches. They are issues that would require significant changes among the participating parties. Note: It is likely that neither the Evangelical Lutherans nor the Episcopalians could or would be party to a merger with parties that hold to a differing view of ordained ministry.

5.   There are behavioral expectations of both laymen and clergy associated with churches in the fundamentalist/evangelical traditions. Similar behavioral expectations may be found in Pentecostal churches and among modern-day Gnostics. They may include counseling of members to avoid:

- Divorce

- The consumption of alcoholic beverages

- Attendance at movies

- Dancing

- Gambling

- Tobacco use

- Attendance at entertainments which portray immoral behavior

Some groups ask members to refrain from drinks that contain caffeine, consuming of meat and meat products (sometimes just pork), saying the Pledge of Allegiance to the US flag, or celebrating certain events, such as Halloween or even Christmas. The proscription of such behaviors by church authorities does not have the power it had in years past. Still, church-authorized behavior and expectations continue to exist with greater or lesser adherence.

All of the above-cited behaviors would be unlikely to be promulgated from a mainline pulpit, although mainline preachers might well counsel moderation in alcohol and tobacco use or gambling.

The hope of many in the evangelical camp that Christians from mainline churches might bond with evangelicals has deep historic roots. At this time in history, it is necessary to conclude that differences of importance exist between the two groups and these differences are likely to frustrate hopes for closer relationships.

What Does the Future Hold for the Mainline Churches?

To this point, we have established that the churches of those denominations characterized as mainline:

1. Have deep roots in the apostolic tradition, the Reformation, and the life of this nation.

2. Have dominated American Protestantism until the relatively recent past.

3. Have traditionally been served by an educated ministry and laity.

4. Have experienced drastic declines in membership over the course of the last five decades.

5. Are now challenged by churches of the Christian right, modern-day Gnostics,

and non- or anti-Christian individuals and organizations.

The questions must be answered: Can the seven mainline denominations and their churches survive? With what kind of membership can they survive and for how long? Should they survive? Can the churches of the mainline regain momentum and, once again, become predominant?

Of course they can survive for the foreseeable future. They are not without significant advantages, veritable bricks in the edifice of continuity. Their most obvious strength is that they have an impressive physical presence throughout the land. Buildings of size, beauty, and permanence characterize local congregations of each of the subject denominations. From nave to chapel, tower to nursery, classrooms to camps, the mainline churches virtually shout, "We are of the establishment. Just look at us! If you want a religious affiliation that reflects your place in society, you must join us." It is a truism that the membership of the mainline churches is, or was, comprised of many who are of the establishment.

Whether the physical plants of the churches of the mainstream are of recent origin or ones built a century or more ago, their facilities are substantial, and they are downright ubiquitous. Steeples and towers reach to the heavens, punctuating the landscape for miles around. Spread across the land in cities, suburbs, and open country, their very presence bespeaks endurance.

Think of virtually any American city, and there they are—the buildings of the mainline churches—in Boston on Copley Plaza, in New York on Fifth Avenue and Wall Street and in Morningside Heights, in Cleveland at University Circle, and in Los Angeles on the Miracle Mile and MacArthur Park. It is a kind of bricks-and-mortar evangelism those buildings perform, "Come to Jesus! We're right here. Just come on in!"

But for some, there is something foreboding about these ecclesiastical outcroppings. Their size, their beauty, their prominence all make it difficult for some to walk through their doors. Whether lonely, grief-stricken, addicted, hungry, or addled, some find these physical manifestations of the mainline off-putting, preferring rather to present themselves and the challenges of their lives to those organizations whose message is proclaimed in a store front or a repurposed industrial facility or the multi-building modern campus of the megachurch. The buildings of the mainstream may seem advantageous but are not always so.

Another plus for the churches in the mainstream, at least some of them, is that they are in possession of significant financial resources. Many of those churches have been around for decades, not a few can claim more than a century of life. In that time, some have acquired significant resources: bequests and annuities have funded endowments and trusts. A not inconsiderable number of the mainline congregations are well funded and are not dependent totally on the annual stewardship drive for funds to pursue ministry and mission.

However, the reduced membership which marks the mainline churches today has caused many to face financial challenges they might have thought unlikely just a few years ago. Fewer people in the pews usually mean fewer dollars in the offering plates. Some of the shortfall is made up by increased giving on the part of loyal members. The Episcopal Church has recently shown that the number of members is down over 10 percent in the last ten years. However, pledging per giving unit is now at an all-time high—an average of $2,190 a year. A related and troubling fact is that the average age of members is similarly at an all-time high. Notwithstanding endowments and increased generosity on the part of fewer members, churches of the mainline denominations must anticipate greater challenges, resulting in deeper budget cuts.

There are other resource issues: those lovely buildings were rarely constructed with long-term maintenance needs in mind. Those needs can be, often are, expensive, sometimes prohibitively so. Similarly, operations in the building(s) of mainstream Protestantism can bleed dry even the well-financed church: the cost of utilities and repairs, staff salaries and benefits,[46] educational and music expenses take a fearsome toll on resources that, inevitably, will grow.

All of that is happening as the venerable churches of the mainline denominations are facing the reality that they are situated in neighborhoods in which residents, by reason of inherited culture or ethnicity, will prefer churches of other persuasions. Earlier, we noted that many churches in the inner city have struggled mightily and effectively to serve the needs of those living in proximity to the church premises. In such cases, these factors are almost always present: the worshiping, giving, leading members participate from residences that are distant from the church building. The close-at-hand persons served by the churches are rarely able to be the major source of financial support. The result? Income from invested funds or dependence on the gifts of nonresident members is required to support the ministry; the long-term trend of local membership gifts is clearly downward.

Those factors have driven many mainline churches to relocate to the suburbs. As noted earlier, the ironic reality is that some churches that moved from "downtown" to a site farther out some forty years ago are currently facing yet another move due to a new population shift.

Another asset the mainline churches bring to the future is the educational level of their leadership. Pastors have, at minimum, seven years of post-secondary education and growing numbers have added an additional two or three years (cf. D. Min. degrees) to address, in an academically structured program of study, the concrete challenges of ministry in today's world. The pastor's work is undergirded by knowledge of the Bible, of history, of theology, of psychology, of ethics, and more recently, of sociology and management. They ought to be able to think circles around their putative competitors. For whatever reasons, they may not be able to out-motivate their challengers. The exercise of reason is not always what the spiritually hungry are seeking.

Similarly, the lay leadership found in mainline churches is, not infrequently, reflective of the very best of the American middle and upper middle class. By way of illustration, we have come upon a historic mainline church, of modest size, located in one of the poorest zip codes in its state which has mounted a vibrant ministry of service to its communities, whose membership rolls include judges, doctors, lawyers, professors, contractors, teachers, experts in information technology, etc., most of whom reside at a distance from the church property. The quality of such lay leadership is dazzling and is likely to be found infrequently in churches of the right or in the Gnostic congregations. Is it just a matter of time before established, quality lay leadership takes itself to an evangelical church? Or will that quality leadership prove, somehow, to be the salvation of the mainline churches?

Statistical studies show that mainline church members and leaders are older (nearly a quarter are over sixty-five years of age), predominantly white (91 percent), relatively well-to-do (36 percent with an annual income in excess of $75,000), well educated (34 percent have graduated from college or have a graduate degree), and without children in the home (70 percent).[47]

With a grand physical plant, relatively ample financial resources, a history of significant accomplishment, an educated ministry, and a skilled and committed lay cadre, what is lacking? Why have the mainline churches diminished in size and influence?

First, the message preached by churches in growth mode is clear, straightforward, and compelling. Their message is that there is life after death and that each person will be judged after they have departed this life. Those who have been saved—that is, those who have accepted Jesus as Lord and Savior—will have their sins forgiven and will live. Those who are not saved will be punished for their sins.

The message as proclaimed by the mainline's competitors admits to no subtlety, no complexity, no confusion. It is repeated over and over; it is not uncommon for each service of worship to conclude with an invitation. "If you want to have everlasting life with Jesus, come forward as a sign of your commitment to Jesus." As the choir (or congregation) sings "Just As I Am" or a similar call to decision, attendees at the service, presumably visitors and nonmembers (if one is a member, he/she has presumably made this decision) step into the aisle and move to the front of the sanctuary, where they are met by the minister and one or more deacons or other church officials. Greetings are exchanged, tears may flow, arrangements are made for a private counseling session, and the gates of heaven are figuratively flung open.

This is powerful stuff! It really is. And for those who have never seen or experienced the invitation and response in a fundamentalist or evangelical service, it may be difficult to understand the deep feelings engendered when the members of congregation see salvation enacted. A member of an evangelical megachurch, in giving good marks to her minister, recently said to me with great feeling, "He has a real passion for the lost." She knew what it was like to see a lost soul enter into the love of God.

Some scholars, not all of whom are students of religions, attribute the growth of Christianity in the first and second centuries to the promise of life after death. The myths of Greece and Rome, for the most part, pictured a dark and gloomy afterlife, if they pictured one at all—the boatman and the River Styx, etc. Hebrew religion promised no afterlife for individuals until rather late in its history. They embraced, instead, the idea that one might live on through the life of the nation. The later writings do speak of an afterlife but in general, almost antiseptic terms.

In the centuries before Jesus, there grew up in the ancient Near East, a group of religions known as mystery religions which promised that one who had been initiated into the mysteries would survive death. These religions were especially popular with the men of the Roman legions and of the Greek and Egyptian and other armies. Facing death was what those men did; it was their occupation. That they wanted to survive death was understandable. Primitive Christianity has been categorized by many scholars as a mystery religion. Paul's message, and Peter's, and the message of other of the early missionaries were ones of salvation for those who confessed Jesus. Salvation meant eternal bliss, life after death with Jesus Christ. Thus, the early church grew and prospered.

It is not that the churches of the mainline deny or argue with the idea of life after death. And it is not that commitment to Christ is a small thing. It is, rather, that many of their clergy concentrate their message on life—that is, what it is like to live as a Christian in this life. Here, now, one finds meaning, a sense of spiritual well-being and participation in true community with others of the faith. Here, today, one knows forgiving love. Here, one is empowered to act to make the world a better place, to struggle for peace, to fight poverty, to heal the broken. Here, one can experience the holy.

Now all of that is good stuff. It too is powerful. And it is also faithful to the message of Jesus and his apostles. But for many, it is not as motivational as a message that declares, "We can snatch you from the fires of hell. We can do it right now." And that's what the mainline church's competitors promise.

The result is that some studies suggest that the churches of the right are approaching 50 percent of the population of the United States. They are younger (fewer than one-fifth of the members of evangelical churches are over sixty-five years of age; Mormons and Jehovah's Witnesses trend younger still). They are not as well-to-do as the membership of the mainline churches, have fewer years of schooling, and are more diverse. Witnesses are much more diverse—only 48 percent are white and are far more likely to be in a family setting that includes children.[48]

Definitively, the message proclaimed by the Christian right and the modern-day Gnostic churches that you can be assured of life after death and salvation from punishment in hell is one reason for the growth of those churches. The message of the mainline, as it is heard by those outside the church, be good and grow spiritually, pales in comparison.

The American Religious Survey of 2008 found that all sections of the country since 1990 have gained in numbers of persons reporting that they have no religion. New England, the historic home of three of the mainline denominations, showed the greatest drop in religious affiliations; twenty-two percent of the respondents claimed no religion, up by 14 percent since 1990. The Pacific region (California, Oregon, and Washington) showed the second largest drop—20 percent. On a national scale, the Pew Forum reports that nearly one in five men claim no religion affiliation, compared with about 13 percent of women.

Alongside the power of their message and the fact that the churches of the right are comprised of members who are significantly younger than those of the mainline churches, another of their competitive advantages is that they seem to be more in tune to their age. The clergy of the right know and make use of Facebook, MySpace, YouTube, hip-hop music, and rap. They are not captive to the ancient (and let's face it) aristocratic-aesthetic of the denominational hymn books, prayers, and vestments. Improvisation in prayer and sermon serve to communicate spontaneity and warmth and sometimes attain levels that can only be described as artistic. Shirt sleeves are rolled-up; collars are unbuttoned; slang words punctuate sermons. What formerly constituted dignity and appropriateness in the conduct of services in the mainline churches now seems stuffy, formal, stand-offish, insincere, and old-fashioned.

If the music in the churches of mainline competitor's—praise music—seems to have more in common with a vacuous ditty such as Disneyland's *It's a Small World After All* than with Luther's *A Mighty Fortress is Our God*, well, "the kids like it" and so do their parents. The uplift the Christian right strives to create in worship music is constituted of enthusiasm and positive themes. Music in a minor key is not for them, at least not in worship. And the guitars, drums, and tambourines create the musical ambiance that many of the young "dig."

It is easy for the mainline churches to criticize, but the simple truth is that those churches of the mainline's competitors have changed lives. Here is a mother who was addicted to hard drugs, who had five children by four men and three aborted pregnancies by three men, all of whom were different from those who had fathered her children. She found Christ in a fundamentalist church, became clean, a devoted mother married to the man who fathered her last child, who now holds a highly responsible job in county government. There is nothing to criticize about that! That is not shallow. That woman did not turn her life around as a result of the efforts of a mainline church, its pastors, or lay leaders. It was a church of the Christian right that reached out to her and, in keeping with the ways of Jesus, helped her change her life! There are more such stories of the power of Christian witness than can be counted, stories of real people whose broken lives have been made whole by the ministry of churches of the right.

And here is the very point at which the mainline churches differ from the fundamentalists, evangelicals, and modern-day Gnostics: the message of the latter promises salvation for the individual, the message of the other commits the mainstream to work for social justice. The Protestant churchmen and churchwomen who marched for civil rights with Martin Luther King were overwhelmingly men and women of the main-line churches (by way of setting the record straight, there were lots of Jews and Catholics who marched too). They were soldiers in the war on poverty. They struggled to help the nation free itself from the tragedy that was the Vietnam War. And today, they are green; they stand for a comprehensive and generous national immigration policy; they want to bring home the sol-diers; they work for universal health care.

While the Christian right is roundly criticized for "mixing religion and politics," the Christian main-stream also has a political agenda. The differences are in the content of their respective agendas: for the fundamentalists and evangelicals, it tends to be anti-abortion, anti-gay, anti-stem cell research, etc.; for the mainstream, it is pro-immigration reform, clean energy, peace, health care reform, etc.

Fairness requires acknowledgement of the fact that a growing number of leaders of the Christian right are beginning to address, in both word and deed, the need for social justice: Jim Wallis in Washington, DC, and Rick Warren in Orange County, California, are but two of many evangelicals who are speaking with a prophetic voice to our nation's ills.

The advantages and problems of the mainline churches and their competitors may be charted.

The Churches of the Mainline

Advantages	Challenges
1. Widespread physical presence	1. The buildings are aging and require costly maintenance
2. Financial resources: endowments, member generosity	2. Memberships have been declining for at least four decades
3. Professional leadership is well-educated; similarly, lay leadership is well-schooled	3. Fewer people = reduced financial resources
4. The message preached has power	4. Members are older, have fewer children
5. Are perceived to be of the establishment	5. Show little understanding of or appreciation for contemporary culture
6. Have a long and distinguished history	6. Message is not as compelling as that of their competitors
	7. Often proclaim a wishy-washy theology.

The Churches of the Christian Right

Advantages	Challenges
1. Their message is compelling to large numbers of people	1. Clergy and laity tend not to be so highly educated
2. They are widespread and are widely publicized in the media—note the mega-church movement	2. Their physical presence is often hidden
3. They have been in rapid growth mode	3. Members tend to come from a lower social and economic class
4. Membership is relatively young; they tend to attract youth	4. Have strongly identified with the Republican Party and its program
5. Their emphasis on individuals—changes lives for the better	5. Are frequently identified with anti-science attitudes
6. They are very clear about their authority—the Bible	6. Clergy discipline is sporadic
7. There is understanding of and appreciation for the modern world	

DUANE L. DAY

The Mainline Comes Back?

Can the mainline churches reverse their forty-plus year decline and again become relevant on the American religious scene? If so, what are the changes they must embrace in program, style, and message?

They must seek guidance from those who have demonstrated that they know "how to do" church growth. Right now, the churches of the Christian right are the experts in the membership development arena. Yet astonishingly, the clergy and lay leaders of the historic Protestant denominations are not talking to these experts, asking them how they do it, what tactics they employ to woo members. Instead, mainline churchmen assume a posture that can only be described as smug, convinced as they are of their own intellectual and cultural superiority. The situation calls for a healthy dose of humility on the part of the mainline leadership as they assume the role of students. They have much to learn.

They must give increased attention to the ministries to the young. Church membership statistics are compelling: the members of the mainline churches are significantly older than the members of the churches of the Christian right; the long-term consequences of such data are continued shrinkage. The churches of the mainline must reorder their institutional finances to recruit, hire, and support talented community outreach leaders who understand and can operate within the currents of contemporary youth culture. Such an effort will doubtlessly result in actions at the local church level that have an effect on music in worship, technology, language style, pulpit garb, etc. Those actions may well be difficult for some in the mainline to tolerate, but they could have payoffs in cultural relevance, which may result in membership growth.

They must be willing to add to their efforts on behalf of ministries to persons. The churches of historic Protestantism have been remarkably responsive for at least the last fifty years to the problems of society: racism, poverty, war, hunger, women's rights, etc. And more recently, many of those churches have turned attention to such issues as homosexual rights (gay marriage), environmental causes, comprehensive immigration reform, etc. It is not that mainline churches should turn away from cause-related ministries rather that they remember and also give attention to the needs, the hurts, the challenges, the opportunities faced by individuals. God has words of healing, strength, and comfort for persons, and the mainline churches have not, in recent years, balanced their ministry to society with ministry to persons. Mainline churches are called to reclaim, as their own, the gospel's passion for the lone sinner.

They must take seriously their responsibility to encourage and sustain the sense of community within local congregations. There is abundant evidence that churches in which community exists are churches that can successfully meet and withstand challenges. The recent Towers Watson research study, funded by the United Methodists, identified the existence of thriving small groups as one of the marks of a "vital" local congregation. (The other marks they identified were a pastor who supports his/her laity, relevant preaching in worship services that have contemporary significance, and quality lay leadership.) Ours is an age which salutes large and celebrates huge. If community is to exist within the local congregation, and if the sense of community is to be of sufficient strength to undergird membership growth, then *small, intimate* circles of members must be set in place to nurture the cohesion which marks community.

They must take with renewed seriousness the education of their members. As noted earlier, it is evident that the mainline's competitors do the more compelling job of educating their members. The Bible is often presented as having an answer to every question. Mainline churches, on the other hand, are comprised of too many members who believe and who say, "All religions are alike." That statement and the attitude behind it is simply wrong and their pastors know it, but those very pastors are not doing a good job of teaching their flocks the commitments which are at the heart of the historic Protestant churches and what those commitments have to do with day-to-day lives of their members or prospective members. The fact is the mainline churches have, at root, nothing to be ashamed of in the realms of theology, biblical knowledge and understanding and history. Their contributions to individuals and society are powerful and deserving of the attention of their fellow Christians. The mainline pastors need to take on, as a personal responsibility, the job of educating their members about what it is that their churches stand for and what it is they have to offer.

They will be significantly advantaged by embarking on programs supportive of spiritual growth. The Christian Church has always been most vital when it has been marked by the conviction that God and man/woman are, or may be, in communication with one another. Such was characteristic of American churches during the First and Second Great Awakenings. And such was the mark of the church in the first century, during the Reformation and in the growth of the Pentecostal and Charismatic movements. To work for spiritual growth does not have to mean speaking in tongues or prophesying. It will mean that mainline church members will be encouraged to make time for private prayers, silence, listening, fasting, and retreats or some combination of those practices. Openness to God's voice to seeking a personal relationship with the

All Merciful One will strengthen the faithful which, in turn, will empower the mainline church's ministries.

The strategies for mainline church renewal may be summarized:

- Seek the advice and counsel of those who have had success in promoting church growth. Do so with humility.

- Make a strategic decision to emphasize ministry to the young.

- Give renewed attention to ministry to individuals and their personal needs.

- Mount tactical initiatives designed to build community with the local congregation.

- Make the education of members a priority. How do we see God at work in this congregation?

- Promote spiritual growth among members—personal prayer, silence, fasting, listening to the voice of God.

If the mainline churches do not change both tactics and strategy in order to halt membership decline and reenter growth mode, some conclusions about their near and midterm future are clear.

1. They will survive but as smaller, less powerful entities. The age of their members argues for shrinking—albeit not to the point of extinction. Their history, their physical presence, their financial stature, their establishment connections pretty much assures that the preponderance of the mainline denominations will enter the twenty-second century as more or less viable institutions. One can expect changes in programmatic emphases; the adoption of specific spiritual disciplines appears to be one direction those emphases might go, ministry to immigrant populations another.

2. The coming years will see the rise of issues that may sunder the denominations and many local churches. The most obvious such issue right now focuses on matters that have to do with homosexuality: What about gay marriage? Should gays be eligible for ordination? How will decisions about those matters impact local churches of the mainline as they relate to their brothers and sisters in other lands and on other continents?

Clearly decisions made on these and related matters will weaken the bonds of affection mainline Christians have for one another. The Episcopal Church, subsequent to the consecration of openly gay Gene Robinson as bishop of New Hampshire, has experienced widespread defections of conservative parishes and their affiliation with overseas Anglican dioceses. The election of two women priests, one of whom is openly lesbian, as assistant bishops in the diocese of Los Angeles has exacerbated the problem.

In one way or another, almost all of the mainline denominations are struggling with questions having to do with the relationship of the Christian churches to homosexuals. The United Church of Christ may be the exception; at some level, it appears to have put those questions to rest. It may be no coincidence that its membership has declined by a greater percentage than any of the other mainline denominations.

Faith commitments ought not to be made, or worked out, on the basis of poll results. Still, it is informative that a recent survey found that 56 percent of all mainline Protestants believe that homosexuality should be accepted by the general public, while only 26 percent of evangelicals agreed.

The issue is not the only one that sets apart the mainline denominations. There will be others: clean energy, climate change, and comprehensive immigration reform are all on the horizon.

3. It can be anticipated that in the near future there may be—almost certainly *will* be— some mergers of two or more of the denominations of the mainline, perhaps others. The United Church of Christ, the American Baptists, and the Disciples of Christ are the most likely candidates for merger; they are the smallest of the seven. The UCC and

the Disciples are already in a relationship that has grown beyond mere conversations; the ABC could join in those processes but may be more likely to find a home with other Baptists or a yet-to-be formed "non-denominational" or interdenominational federation.

It would appear that the Methodists, the Episcopalians, and the Evangelical Lutherans might suffer the least from attrition in the coming years, although they are all wrestling with homosexual issues. The Methodists are so large that even shrinkage of three-fourths will leave them with a substantial core. In addition, their connectional structure (read: structured authority) could admit to management decision-making for strategic advantage.

The histories and liturgical nature of the Episcopalians and Evangelical Lutherans argue for continuity. Although they are both connectional, in neither case does their structure provide the explicit power of Methodist connectionalism—still, issues of institutional life and death may empower their respective Presiding Bishops to engage in the strategic decision making the coming decades are sure to require.

The Presbyterians are a conundrum. Although they have a well-defined governance structure, that structure is ponderous, at best. Further, Presbyterians, by reason of their structure, are having difficulty even taking hold of the homosexual issues. They depend, for denominational action, on the positions taken by their constituent presbyteries. There are 173 of them; sectional/regional differences and related theological proclivities play an important role in the attitudes and votes of many of the presbyteries. The national church will wait on those decisions.

As the mainline churches shrink, both in size and influence, we may expect that changes will occur in the composition of their membership. Throughout much of the preceding four centuries, community leaders (along with state and national leaders) have been drawn to one or another of the mainline denominations. Of US presidents, eleven have been Episcopalians, ten Presbyterians, five Methodists, three Disciples of Christ, and two Congregationalists—that is, thirty-one of forty-two presidents (almost three-fourths) have, for at least a time, belonged to one of the churches we have identified as mainline.[49] Of the 535 members of the two houses of Congress in 2009, 46 percent claimed membership in a mainline church.[50]

That has been, in large measure, a function of the establishment nature of the mainline churches in American society. Political leadership aside, much of the business and education leadership of the nation have made their way to one or another of the mainline churches.[51]

As the evangelical churches and modern-day Gnostic churches grow in numbers and stature relative to the mainline, we may reasonably expect to see growing numbers of the powerful being attracted to those churches.

4. The churches of the historic mainline denominations may be expected to adopt some of the tactics and practices of their competitors. That is a trend that is already established: lighter, more "hip" music utilized in worship; popular instrumentation replacing dependence on piano and organ; video screens showing the preacher and musicians; PowerPoint sermons; Facebook and Twitter (and their successors) freely utilized by the membership; growing utilization of the ideas and services of younger and younger members; reduced usage of clerical clothing and vestments.

5. Because of the compelling nature of the salvation message, as proclaimed by the fundamentalists and evangelicals, it can be anticipated that some preachers, squarely in the mainstream, will place emphasis in their ministries on personal transformation and the promise of life after death for those who confess Jesus as Lord and Savior. It has been, until now, a topic addressed most frequently in mainline churches only at Easter. That is a failure of significance; the Christian gospel has, at its core, Jesus's resurrection and of life with him for those confessing his name. Another failure of the mainline has to do

with reluctance to talk about, indeed to own up to, the reality of sin. Reinhold Niebuhr, through the 1930s, set his message within the context of nonviolence and pacifism. By the 1940s, he had come to understand that evil as represented and acted out by such as Adolf Hitler was within the potential of every human and he turned to an acknowledgement of the reality of sin and to condemn sin in all its guises. Mainline clergy and theologians have largely ignored the reality of sin.

Change, the universal challenge with which every human enterprise must deal, is being thrust on the church—those of the mainline and those of the right. It is appropriate that we celebrate the manifold gifts the mainline churches have brought to our common life—everything from separation of church and state and abolitionism to civil rights and the empowerment of women. Ubiquitous are the institutions and accomplishments of the mainline on the map of this nation: colleges and universities, hospitals, books and their publishing companies, arts and music, youth programs and ministries to the poor and outcast, scholarships and scholarly research.

Yet even as we acknowledge the good the mainline has done, we need also to own up to the fact that the actions of the mainline have not always been on the side of righteousness. Perhaps the fifty-year decline of the mainline should be seen as God's punishment on the religious expressions of the American establishment. And perhaps the decline is nothing more than the never-ending cycle of decay that follows growth and leads to new forms of life.

Whatever it is, let us thank God for the gifts the mainline churches have brought the nation and pray that the coming manifestations of Christ's church will preserve and move beyond the best of those accomplishments. And let us beg forgiveness for those actions which have not been faithful responses to the Good News of Christ. Similarly, let us praise the Christian right for their commitment to personal redemption and spiritual growth. May the mainline churches acknowledge that the conversion experience may mark the beginning of new life in Christ.

Preaching about sin and salvation will doubtlessly bring the mainline churches closer to their competition. Notwithstanding, there are few mainline clergy with whom I am acquainted who are prepared to announce God's everlasting punishment of sinners who have not had the salvation experience.

Respectfully, let us ask God to grant the gift of humility to all those who claim the name of Christ that we may, learning from one another, share mission and ministry.

Endnotes

Back in the Day

1   He never played down his Catholicism; he appeared
    in clerical regalia and began each show by writing
    "JMJ" on his blackboard, explaining that the initials
    stood for Jesus, Mary, and Joseph.

2   "Findings" from National Council of Churches of
    Christ in the USA, (NCCCUSA), 2010 Yearbook
    of American and Canadian Churches.

3   It is important to note that rabbis and other Jewish
    leaders were deeply committed to and involved in
    the civil rights movement. Fundamentalist and
    Evangelical leaders, in the 1960s, were all too rarely
    to be found on the front lines in the civil rights
    struggle.

4   On being interviewed by a California university administrator about the students he was recruiting on campus, Chuck Smith, the founder of the Calvary Chapel movement, said, "We'll get them with guitars and tambourines" and, to a remarkable degree, he did.

5   It is music sometimes referred to, even by its proponents, as 7-11 music—seven words repeated eleven times.

6   Andover graduate Adoniram Judson set out to convert Burma to Congregational Orthodoxy, only to become convinced that the Baptists were right about believer's baptism. He declared himself a Baptist and proclaimed the gospel in Burma and won converts for many years.

7   Finney also had a strong commitment to the social dimensions of Christian faith. Christian abolitionists grew up during the Second Great Awakening. Temperance societies were formed. The women's movement had roots deep in the religion of experience.

8   *New York Times*, Book Review, April 26, 2009, Hanna Rosin, p. 14.

Christian Fundamentalism

9   It is noteworthy that the term *fundamentalist* is now applied in many non-Christian settings—it is common and accepted practice to speak of Islamic fundamentalism and even fundamentalist Marxists.

10 As a five-year-old, this author was urged by a visiting evangelist to sign a pledge not to attend motion pictures. He did and, due to his parents' belief that he should keep his word, it was a pledge he kept until midway through high school.

11 In 1925, the convention adopted a formal confession of faith, "The Baptist Faith Message." Baptists have generally stood in opposition to creeds.

12 Elliott's book had been published by Broadman Press, a creature of the Baptist Sunday School Board. *The Message of Genesis* was withdrawn from circulation, and Elliott was fired by Midwestern Seminary.

The Evangelicals/Neo-Evangelicals

13 When Andover Theological Seminary was founded in 1807 as the nation's first graduate school of theology, it was a response to Unitarianism, which had "captured" Harvard University. One early description of Andover, c.1810, refers to the school as "orthodox."

14 Although Billy Graham is usually credited with founding *Christianity Today*, it is clear that a number of thoughtful evangelicals were involved in its birth.

15   *Christianity Today International* currently publishes nine magazines and newsletters, this after closing down the publication of four magazines due to problems associated with costs.

16   Adopted by the Board of Directors of the National Association of Evangelicals, October 7, 2004; reaffirmed by the board in March 2007.

17   Gallup polls between 1976 and 2000 identified evangelicals as having 33 percent to 47 percent of the United States population.

Pentecostalists and Charismatics

18   Some sources are more conservative in Pentecostalist membership projections: one sets the number of adherents worldwide at 130 million. Other sources suggest that as many as 25 percent of the Christians in the world are Pentecostalists.

19   Notable among early non-Methodist supporters of Christian holiness was Asa Mahan, president of Oberlin College, and evangelist Charles Finney.

20   The theological proposition that man has freedom to act for or against God. It is based on the work of Jacob Arminius, who denied predestination. Arminianism has often been seen as a force for morality and transformation.

Modern-Day Gnostics

21 This sentence is not to be taken to mean that no Gnostic manuscripts were known until recently. Many of the Gnostic writings have been known for more than 1500 years.

22 The Nicene Creed.

23 They are not the only ones to do so. Some other religious entities engage in the same or similar practice.

24 The women are relatively new to the mission years.

25 Jews do not pronounce the name; when they come across it in reading, they typically substitute the title, Adonai, Lord.

26 *Yearbook of Jehovah's Witnesses*, 2009 edition.

27 "A Position Statement on the Vegetarian Diet," adopted by the General Conference of Seventh-Day Adventists Nutrition Council.

Atheists, Agnostics, and Secularists

28 Pew Forum on Religion and Public Life, Statistics on Religion in America Report, Report 1: Religious Affiliation. http://religious.pewforum.org/reports

29 Sam Harris, *Letter to a Christian Nation* (New York: Alfred A. Knoph, 2006).

30   David Brook, "The Neural Buddhists," (*The New York Times*, May 13, 2008).

31   Richard Dawkins, *The God Delusion*, p. 81.

32   W. K. Clifford, "The Ethics of Belief" in *Lectures and Essays* (London: MacMillan, 1879), p. 18.

33   Lord Kelvin, "Electrical Limits of Measurement," 1883.

34   Pew Forum on Religion and Public Life, Religion and Public Life, Statistics on Religion in America Report, Report 1, Religious Affiliation. http://religious.pewforum.org/reports

35   Bertrand Russell, "Am I An Atheist or An Agnostic?" pamphlet, 1947.

Why Did They Go?

36   The Pew Forum on Religion and Public Life issued a report in 2010 that says atheists, Jews, Mormons, and Evangelical Christians are all more knowledgeable about their faith than mainline Protestants.

37   Johnson, Hoge, and Ludens' 1995 study on the Mainline Churches: "The Real Reason for Decline."

38   "Did You Really Go to Church This Week? Behind The Poll Data," *Christian Century*, May 6, 1998, pp. 472-475.

39   Moore & Day, *Urban Church Breakthrough* (Harper & Row: New York, 1966).

40   William M. Chace in "The Decline of the English Department" (*The American Scholar*, Autumn 2009), pp. 32-42.

The More We Get Together

41   The National Council of Churches, which has been one of the primary forms the ecumenical impulse has taken for the mainline churches in the United States, is now a troubling entity for many former supporters—social and political issues are proving divisive.

42   When the provisional structure of World Council of Churches was prepared in 1938, just months before the outbreak of World War II, the basis of the council, as adopted, was "The World Council of Churches is a fellowship of churches which accept the Lord Jesus Christ as God and Savior."

43   Billy Graham made that very argument.

44   *The Christian Century*, June 2, 2009, Volume 126, No. 11, page 40.

45   It should be noted that most Southern Baptist churches are committed to an ordination procedure that is not unlike the procedure followed by American Baptist churches.

What Does the Future Hold for the Mainline Churches?

46   A recent news report noted that the annual sal-
       ary and benefits package for the senior minister of
       a well-known, large mainline church amounted to
       $600,000. The minister resigned when that fig-
       ure and some other facts about the ministry were
       published.

47   Pew Forum on Religion and Public Life, Portrait
       and Demographics of United States Religious
       Affiliation. http://religiouns.pewforum.org/portraits

48   Ibid.

The Mainline Comes Back?

49   See DeGregorio, Wm. A., *The Complete Book of
       U.S. Presidents* (2nd edition). (New York: Dembner
       Books, 1989).

50   James L. Evans, "Spirituality of Members of
       Congress," published 10 December 2006 in the
       Decatur Daily.

Index